international thai cooking

NUTRITIOUS THAI DISHES

Sangdad Books

National Library of Thailand Cataloging in Publication Data
NUTRITIOUS THAI DISHES.--4th ed.--Bangkok : Sangdad, 2004.
104 p.
1. Cookery, Thai. I. Title.
641.59593
ISBN : 974-7160-12-9

NUTRITIOUS THAI DISHES

First Published, October 1994
Second Published, August 1998
Third Published, November 2001
Fourth Published, July 2004

Consultant Sisamon Kongpan
Director Nidda Hongwiwat
Editor Nalin Khu-Armornpatana
English Editor Richard Goldrick
Editor's Assistant Obchoel Imsabai
Photography & Design Samart Sudto
Layout Rungrudee Panichsri
Illustration Sarayut Yoosuk
Marketing Director Nan Hongvivatana
e-mail : marketing@sangdad.com
Production Director Jiranan Tubniem
e-mail : production@sangdad.com
Printer A.T. Printing Co., Ltd.
Tel. (662) 211-6956

Published and Distributed by Sangdad Publishing Co., Ltd.
320 Lat Phrao 94 (Town in Town) Wangthonglang, Bangkok 10310, Thailand.
Tel. (662) 934-4413, 934-4418-20 ext. 101
Fax. (662) 538-1499
www.sangdad.com
e-mail : sdbooks@sangdad.com

PREFACE

Thai food is becoming more and more popular internationally, gaining recognition as one of the world's great cuisines, because it is delicious, whole some, and easy to cook. To serve the rapidly expanding number of admirers of Thai food in all parts of the world, the Racipe Development Section of Sangdad, Thailand's largest publisher of cookbooks, has done extensive research, compiling more than 5,000 recipes for both traditional and contemporary Thai dishes, and now offers a selection of these in the Easy Cooking Series.

Thai food is not only highly appetizing but very nutritious as well. For this volume, the editor has chosen dishes that are low in fat and nutritionally well balanced. *Nutritious Thai Dishes* presents carefully selected recipes which are easy to prepare and which meet a variety of dietary needs, as indicated in the Introduction. This makes it easy for you to choose the dishes best suited to your health.

With Easy Cooking *Nutritious Thai Dishes,* you can now enjoy your favorite healthful Thai foods at home more often. A little practice in the art of Thai cooking will bring you and your loved ones delightful dining and better health.

Nidda Hongwiwat
Managing Director

INTRODUCTION

Nowadays the concept of eating for healthy living is spreading across the globe, for it has been found that the cause of many health problems lies in improper diet.

Nutritious Thai Dishes presents foods that help maintain health and strength. They are of particular value for people with high blood cholesterol levels, high blood pressure, or other heart and circulatory problems as well as for people who are overweight and those who suffer from constipation.

Fish is a type of food which is appetizing and can be prepared in a wide variety of ways. It is a low-fat source of easily digestible protein and essential amino acids and also provides vitamins, for the oil in fish is high in vitamins A and D. Sea fish are rish in minerals, particularly iodine.

Fish can be divided into three groups on the basis of oil content :

1. Fish with little or no oil are those whose edible flesh has a fat content of less that two percent. The meat of these fish tends to be white. This group includes sea perch grouper, flounder, and squid.
2. Fish with a medium amount of oil have a fat content of between two and five percent. Spanish mackerel, serpent-head, and pony fish are in this group.
3. Oily fish have a fat content of eight percent or more. Their flesh tends to be yellowish.In this group are catfish, salmon, and herring.

Eggs are a valuable food. The protein in hen's eggs is complete, containing all the essential amino acids. Egg yolk is a good source of iron, vitamin A, calcium, and phosphorus.

Yuba is produced from soybeans and so is rich in protein, calcium, and phosphorus.

Cashews are dried nuts which supply high energy. They have medium amounts of protein and carbohydrates and a high amount of phosphorus, necessary for healthy bones and teeth.

Bean curd is made from soybeans. It is a rich source of protein, is readily digestible, and contains no cholesterol. It also provides mineral, especially calcium and phosphorus for strong bones and teeth.

Mushrooms are a type of plant with a high protein content and also provide vitamins and minerals. It has been found that mushrooms are a good food for people with high blood pressure and those who have diseases of the heart, liver, or kidneys. Mushrooms are also held to assist in preventing cancer.

Vegetables provide vitamins and minerals and also contain fiber, of which there is little or none in most other types of food. Eating vegetables thus assists the functioning of the digestive system and helps prevent constipation.

The various types of vegetables contain different amounts of vitamins and minerals. Chinese kale is high in vitamin A. Tomatoes are rish in carotene, which the body converts into vitamin A. Green beans and carrots are also good sources of vitamin A, and carrots contain vitamin C as well. Celery and garlic both have high carotene contents.

The vitamins in vegetables may be lost easily in cooking, and so vegetables should be cooked quickly, for instance, by using little water and high heat, to minimize vitamin loss.

Our cookbook will help you make the dishes that you want and obtain the taste that you like. Knowing about the ingredients you use is a first step toward preparing delicious meals.

Dried shrimp, kung haeng, กุ้งแห้ง, are small shrimp which have been dried in the sun.

Pork kidneys, seng ji, เซ่งจี๊, are bean-shaped organs of the pig having a very strong odor when raw. Before being used in food, they are cut open lengthwise, and the red and

Dried shrimp กุ้งแห้ง

Green beans ถั่วแขก

Chilli sauce ซอสพริก

Dried chilli พริกแห้ง

Fermented soybeans เต้าเจี้ยว

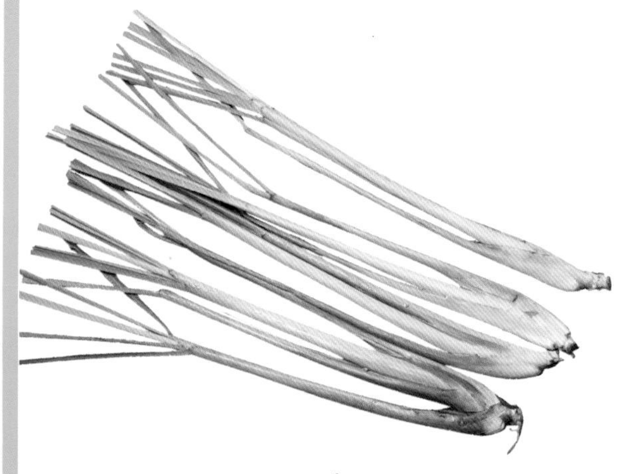

Lemon grass ตะไคร้

Shallot หอมเล็ก

Coriander ผักชี

Sweet basil โหระพา

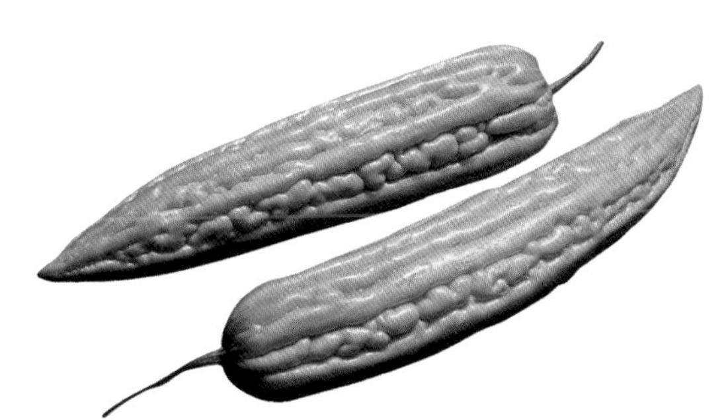

Bitter gourd มะระ

Shiitake mushroom เห็ดหอม

Celery ขึ้นฉ่าย

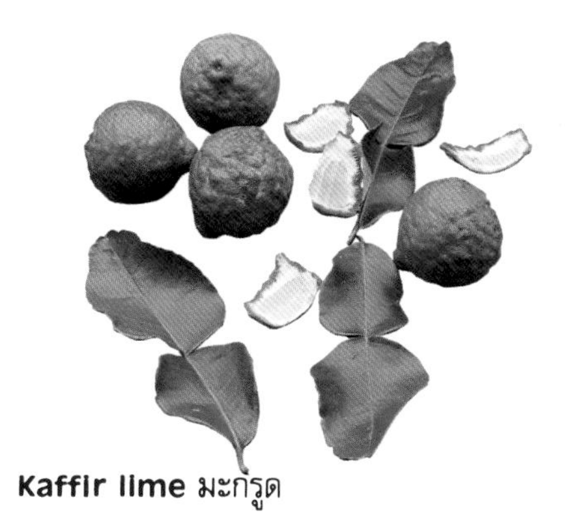

Kaffir lime มะกรูด

white lining is removed. Then they are rubbed with salt and washed until the odor disappears.

Fish sauce, nam pla, น้ำปลา, is a clear, brown liquid derived from a brew of fish or shrimp mixed with salt. It is sold in bottles and plastic jugs as well as in earthenware jars. High quality fish sauce has a fine aroma and taste. Fish sauce is placed on the table as a condiment at nearly every meal, either as is or mixed with sliced chillies and perhaps lime juice.

Oyster sauce, nam man hoi, น้ำมันหอย, is a sweetened soy sauce to which oyster extract is added.

Fermented soybeans, tao jiao, เต้าเจี้ยว, ia a brew of soybeans and salt.

Salted bean, tao si, เต้าซี่, is black beans preserved by salting. The beans are soft and moist, but retain their shape and are packed dry. Fermented soybeans can be substituted.

Light soy sauce, si-iu khao, ซีอิ๊วขาว, is a clear brown liquid used in much the same way that fish sauce is.

Dark soy sauce, si-iu dam, ซีอิ๊วดำ, is opaque, black, viscous, and sweet. It is mixture of soy sauce and molasses.

Brown sugar, nam tan sai daeng, น้ำตาลทรายแดง, or nam tan si ram, น้ำตาลสีรำ, is cane sugar which has not been bleached. The moisture content is high, causing it to form lumps. It has a fresh sugary fragrance and can be used in place of white granulated cane sugar.

Chilli sauce, sot phrik, ซอสพริก, or sot siracha, ซอสศรีราชา, is a prepared sauce something like tobasco sauce and is available in serveral degrees of hotness.

Curry powder, phong ka-ri, ผงกะหรี่, is a prepared mixture of spices such as turmeric, coriander seed, ginger, cloves, cinnamon, mustard, cardamom, cumin, chilli, and salt.

Tapioca Flour, paeng man sampalang, แป้งมันสำปะหลัง, is made from tapioca, or cassava, tubers.

Tapioca pellets, sa-khu met lek, สาคูเม็ดเล็ก, are the tiny balls (about 2 mm. in diameter) made from tapioca.

Lemon grass, ta-khrai, ตะไคร้, *Cymbopgon citratus,* is an aromatic grey-green grass. The bases of the stems are used in cookery.

Kaffir lime, ma-krut, มะกรูด, has green fruit with winkled skin. The rind and the leaves are used in cookery.

Shallot, hom lek, หอมเล็ก, or hom daeng, หอมแดง, *Allium ascalonicum,* is the zesty small red onion favored in Thai cooking.

Sweet basil, horapha, โหระพา, is an attractive plant with deep green leaves and often reddish stems. It has a taste reminiscent of anise.

Spur chilli, phrik chi fa, พริกชี้ฟ้า, have plump fang-like fruits 7-12 cm long. The green immature fruits becomed red, orange, or yellow when ripe. Hot.

Dried chilli, phrik haeng, พริกแห้ง, is fully ripened, red spur chillies dried either in the sun or by smoking. They may be large or small, depending on the variety of spur chilli used. They are prepared by removing the seeds, soaking in water, and then pounding in a mortar.

Coriander, phak chi, ผักชี, *Coriandrum sativum,* is of the parsley family. The leaves and stems are eaten fresh and used frequently as a garnish. The root and the seeds are ingredients in many dishes. The root is taken from the fresh plant. The seeds which are roughly spherical, 2-4 cm in diameter, and range color from off-white to brown, have a pleasant taste and fragrance. They can be bought in the market.

Ginger, khing, ขิง, *Zingiber officinale,* grows from an underground stem, or rhisome. Mature ginger stems are buff colored ; young or fresh ginger, khing on, ขิงอ่อน, is white and is eaten fresh and pickled as well as cooked.'

Galangal, kha, ข่า, *Alpinia galangal,* is a large and lighter-colored relative of ginger and has it own distinctive taste.

Chinese chive flower stalks, dok-kui chai, ดอกกุยช่าย, are the flowers of Chinese chive plants. The green stalks bear white flowers at their tips, They have a sweet flavor and are used in stir-fried dishes.

Green beans, thua khack, ถั่วแขก, are string beans similar to yard-long beans but much shorter in length. They are firm and bright green in color.

Bitter gourd, ma-ra, มะระ, *Momordica charantia,* also called bitter cucumber, carilla fruit, or balsam pear, is an oblong fruit, pointed at one end, which has a handsome pale green surface covered with an irregular pattern of ridges. There are also small dark green varieties.

Celery, kheun chai, ขึ้นฉ่าย, *Apium graveolens,* also called celeriae, turni-prooted celery, or Chinese soup celery, has very small stalks (only a few millimeters across) and a very strong flavor.

Long eggplant, ma-kheua yao, มะเขือยาว, has a long green fruit.

Shiitake mushroom, het hom, เห็ดหอม, is available dried in the market.

Ear mushroom, het hu nu, เห็ดหูหนู, is a dark greyish brown fungus that has a delightful crunchy texture.

TABLE OF CONTENTS

Kung Thot Rat Sot Som

Fried prawns with orange sauce

กุ้งทอดราดซอสส้ม

Ingredients

500 grams medium-sized prawns
1 cup of the juice of Chinese oranges
(som cheng or orange)
1 tbsp. wheat flour
1/2 cup sugar
1/2 tsp. salt
1 cup cooking oil for frying

Preparation

1. Wash, shell, and devein the prawns.
2. Pour the oil into a wok over medium heat. Fry the prawns, and when done, arrange on a plate.
3. Mix in a saucepan the orange juice, sugar, and salt, heat, stir until the sugar dissolves, mix the flour with a little water and add to the pot, continue stirring until the sauce has thickened, and then dip out over the fried prawns.

เครื่องปรุง

กุ้งขนาดกลาง	500	กรัม
ส้มเช้งคั้นน้ำ	1	ถ้วย
แป้งสาลี	1	ช้อนโต๊ะ
น้ำตาลทราย	1/2	ถ้วย
เกลือป่น	1/2	ช้อนชา
น้ำมันสำหรับทอด	1	ถ้วย

วิธีทำ

1. ล้างกุ้ง ปอกเปลือก ผ่าหลังชักเส้นดำออก
2. ใส่น้ำมันสำหรับทอดในกระทะ ทอดกุ้งไฟกลาง ให้สุกเหลือง ตักใส่จาน
3. ผสมน้ำส้ม น้ำตาล เกลือ ตั้งไฟคนให้น้ำตาลละลาย ผสมแป้งสาลีกับน้ำใส่ คนให้เหนียว ตักราดบนตัวกุ้ง

Si Khrong Mu Op Nam Sapparot

Baked spare ribs with pineapple juice

ซี่โครงหมูอบน้ำสับปะรด

Ingredients

1 kilogram tender spare ribs
3 tbsp. finely sliced lemon grass
1 tbsp. finely sliced kaffir lime leaves
5 shallots cut into thin slices
1 tbsp. ground coriander seeds
1/2 cup coconut cream, thickened by boiling
2 tsp. curry powder
1 tbsp. salt
1 cup pineapple juice

Preparation

1. Wash the spare ribs, and chop to separate the ribs into pieces. With a knife, score shallowly the tendon on the bone, and more deeply, the flesh. Then, place the ribs in the pineapple juice to marinate for 10 minutes.
2. Pound the coriander seed, lemon grass, kaffir lime leaf, shallot, and salt together until well ground.
3. Remove the ribs from the pineapple juice, add the mixture from Step 2, the curry powder, and the coconut cream, mix to coat the ribs, and marinate for 30 minutes.
4. Bake the spare ribs in an oven at 400° F. for 20-30 minutes.
5. Serve hot with catsup and fresh vegetables.

เครื่องปรุง

ซี่โครงหมูอ่อน	1	กิโลกรัม
ตะไคร้หั่นฝอย	3	ช้อนโต๊ะ
ใบมะกรูดหั่นฝอย	1	ช้อนโต๊ะ
หอมแดงซอย	5	หัว
ลูกผักชีคั่วป่น	1	ช้อนโต๊ะ
กะทิเคี่ยวข้น ๆ	1/2	ถ้วย
ผงกะหรี่	2	ช้อนชา
เกลือป่น	1	ช้อนโต๊ะ
น้ำสับปะรดคั้น	1	ถ้วย

วิธีทำ

1. ล้างซี่โครงหมูให้สะอาด หั่นเป็นชิ้น ๆ แล้วบั้งซี่โครงตามขวาง ด้านส่วนที่เป็นพังผืดบั้งเป็นปล้อง ๆ หมักกับน้ำสับปะรดประมาณ 10 นาที
2. โขลกลูกผักชี ตะไคร้ ใบมะกรูด หอมแดง เกลือให้ละเอียด
3. เอาซี่โครงหมูขึ้นจากน้ำสับปะรด แล้วเอามาหมักกับเครื่องที่โขลก ใส่ผงกะหรี่ และกะทิเคี่ยวข้นในซี่โครงแล้วหมักต่ออีก 30 นาที
4. นำซี่โครงหมูเข้าอบด้วยไฟ 400 ° ฟ. ประมาณ 20-30 นาที
5. เสิร์ฟร้อน ๆ พร้อมซอสมะเขือเทศ และผักสด

Pla Ma-nao Rat Noei

Fried sea perch with magarine

ปลามะนาวราดเนย

Ingredients

1 half-inch thick sea perch
weighing 500 grams
1 cup carrot, boiled and sliced
1 tsp. salt
1 tbsp. lime juice
2 tsp. margarine
1/2 cup cooking oil for frying

Preparation

1. Dry the fish, rub with the lime juice and salt, and allow to stand for ten minutes or so.
2. Pour the oil into a wok on medium-high heat and fry the fish, turning regularly so it will be tender.
3. When done, remove from the oil, drain, and spread with the margarine while still hot. Serve with the boiled carrot.

เครื่องปรุง

เนื้อปลากะพงขาวหั่น		
หนา 1/2 นิ้ว	500	กรัม
แครอทหั่นชิ้นต้ม	1	ถ้วย
เกลือป่น	1	ช้อนชา
น้ำมะนาว	1	ช้อนโต๊ะ
มาการีน	2	ช้อนชา
น้ำมันสำหรับทอด	1/2	ถ้วย

วิธีทำ

1. ซับปลาให้แห้ง เคล้าปลากับน้ำมะนาวและเกลือ หมักไว้ประมาณ 10 นาที
2. ทอดปลาในกระทะ ไฟปานกลางค่อนข้างแรง พลิกปลากลับไปกลับมา
3. พอสุกตักออก หยอดด้วยมาการีนขณะที่ปลากำลังร้อน เสิร์ฟกับแครอทต้ม

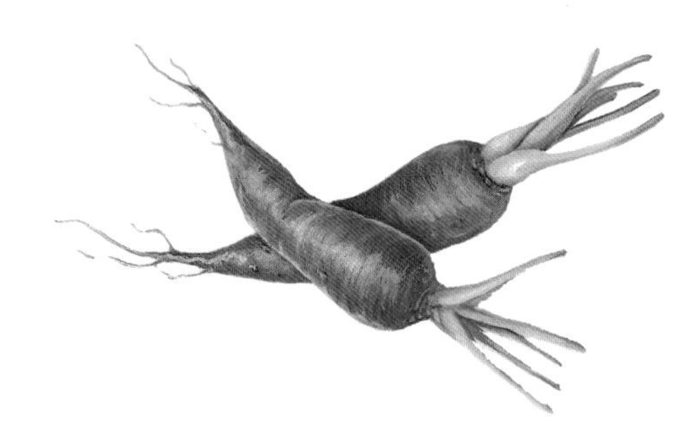

Het Nang Fa Thot

Fried battered mushrooms

เห็ดนางฟ้าทอด

Ingredients

10 Bhutanese oyster mushrooms
1 cup tempura flour
1 cup water
2 cups cooking oil for frying

Preparation

1. Wash the mushrooms and set aside to drain.
2. Mix the flour and water.
3. Heat the oil in a wok. Dip the mushrooms into the batter and then fry golden brown. Remove from the oil and drain on absorbent paper. Serve with chilli sauce.

เครื่องปรุง

เห็ดนางฟ้า	๑๐	ดอก
แป้งทอดกรอบ	๑	ถ้วย
น้ำ	๑	ถ้วย
น้ำมันสำหรับทอด	๒	ถ้วย

วิธีทำ

1. ล้างเห็ดให้สะอาด ผึ่งให้สะเด็ดน้ำ
2. ผสมแป้งกับน้ำ คนให้เข้ากัน
3. ใส่น้ำมันสำหรับทอดในกระทะ เอาเห็ดชุบแป้งทอดให้เหลือง ตักขึ้นวางบนกระดาษซับน้ำมัน เสิร์ฟกับซอสพริก

Het Hom Prung Rot

Seasoned shiitake mushrooms

เห็ดหอมปรุงรส

Ingredients

20 shiitake mushrooms
3 tbsp. sugar
3/4 cup light soy sauce
1 cup of the water in which the mushrooms were soaked
2 cups vegetable oil

Preparation

1. Select large mushrooms. Soak them overnight in water to soften them. Squeeze the water out until they are just damp and then place them in a colander.
2. Heat the oil in a wok. When it is hot, put in the mushrooms and fry until done and fragrant.
3. Remove all but about two table-spoonsful of the oil from the wok
4. Add the soy sauce, sugar, and the cup of the water in which the mushrooms were soaked. Stir fry until the water has evaporated and the sugar and soy sauce have penetrated the mushrooms, and then turn off the heat.

เครื่องปรุง

เห็ดหอม	20	ดอก
น้ำตาลทราย	3	ช้อนโต๊ะ
ซีอิ๊วขาว	3/4	ถ้วย
น้ำแช่เห็ดหอม	1	ถ้วย
น้ำมันพืช	2	ถ้วย

วิธีทำ

1. เลือกเห็ดหอมดอกใหญ่ แช่น้ำค้างคืนไว้ให้นุ่ม เอาเห็ดหอมขึ้น บีบน้ำให้หมาด ใส่กระชอนไว้
2. ใส่น้ำมันในกระทะ ตั้งไฟให้ร้อน ใส่เห็ดหอมลงไปทอดสักครู่ พอเห็ดหอมสุก หอม
3. ตักน้ำมันที่ทอดเห็ดหอมออก ให้เหลือติดกระทะประมาณ 2 ช้อนโต๊ะ
4. ปรุงรสด้วยซีอิ๊วขาว น้ำตาล น้ำแช่เห็ดหอม ผัดจนน้ำแห้ง และเครื่องเข้าเนื้อเห็ดหอมดี ปิดไฟ

Thua Khaek Phat Het

Stir-fried beans and mushrooms

ถั่วแขกผัดเห็ด

Ingredients

100 grams green beans, cut into 2-inch lengths
3 seasoned shiitake mushrooms
4 rice-straw mushrooms, sliced in half
1/2 cup carrot sticks
1/4 cup bite-size pieces of yuba, soaked in water
1/2 tsp. sugar
2 tbsp. light soy sauce
1/4 cup water
2 tbsp. vegetable oil

Preparation

1. Heat the oil in a wok. When hot, put in the beans, both kinds of mushrooms, carrot, yuba, and water and stir fry.
2. Season with the sugar and soy sauce, mix well, and when everything is done, turn off the heat.

Note : seasoned shiitake mushrooms (See page 20)

เครื่องปรุง

ถั่วแขกหั่นยาว 2 นิ้ว	100	กรัม
เห็ดหอมปรุงรส	3	ดอก
เห็ดฟางผ่าครึ่ง	4	ดอก
แครอทหั่นท่อนยาว		
พอคำ	1/2	ถ้วย
ฟองเต้าหู้แช่น้ำ		
หั่นชิ้นพอคำ	1/4	ถ้วย
น้ำตาลทราย	1/2	ช้อนชา
ซีอิ๊วขาว	2	ช้อนโต๊ะ
น้ำ	1/4	ถ้วย
น้ำมันพืช	2	ช้อนโต๊ะ

วิธีทำ

1. ใส่น้ำมันในกระทะ ตั้งไฟให้ร้อน ใส่ถั่วแขก เห็ดหอม เห็ดฟาง แครอท ฟองเต้าหู้ น้ำ
2. ปรุงรสด้วยน้ำตาล ซีอิ๊วขาว ผัดให้ทุกอย่างสุกทั่วกันดี ปิดไฟ

หมายเหตุ เห็ดหอมปรุงรส ดูสูตรเห็ดหอมปรุงรสหน้า 20

Phat Het Hu Nu Ruam Mit

Stir-fried baby corn and ear mushrooms

ผัดเห็ดหูหนูรวมมิตร

Ingredients

1/2 cup ear mushrooms, soaked in water to soften
10 ears baby corn, cut in half lengthwise
100 grams rice-straw mushrooms, halved
1 Chinese soup celery plant, cut into short pieces
1 red and 1 yellow spur chilli, sliced diagonally
1 tsp. sugar
3-4 tbsp. light soy sauce
1/4 cup vegetarian stock
3 tbsp. vegetable oil

Preparation

1. Heat the oil in a wok. When it is hot, put in the ear and rice-straw mushrooms, baby corn, stir fry together, and then add the stock.
2. Season with the sugar and soy sauce and continue stir frying. When everything is done, dip up onto a dish, sprinkle with the celery and chilli, and serve.

เครื่องปรุง

เห็ดหูหนูแช่น้ำให้นิ่ม	1/2	ถ้วย
ข้าวโพดอ่อนหั่นครึ่ง	10	ฝัก
เห็ดฟางผ่าครึ่ง	100	กรัม
ขึ้นฉ่ายหั่นท่อนสั้น	1	ต้น
พริกชี้ฟ้าแดง เหลือง หั่นเฉียง	2	เม็ด
น้ำตาลทราย	1	ช้อนชา
ซีอิ๊วขาว	3-4	ช้อนโต๊ะ
น้ำซุป	1/4	ถ้วย
น้ำมันพืช	3	ช้อนโต๊ะ

วิธีทำ

1. ใส่น้ำมันในกระทะ ตั้งไฟให้ร้อน ใส่เห็ดหูหนู ข้าวโพดอ่อน เห็ดฟาง ผัดให้เข้ากัน ใส่น้ำซุป
2. ปรุงรสด้วยน้ำตาล ซีอิ๊วขาว ผัดพอทั่ว ผักสุก ปิดไฟ ยกลง ตักใส่จาน โรยขึ้นฉ่าย พริก เสิร์ฟ

No Mai Farang Rat Na

Canned asparagus with mushroom sauce

หน่อไม้ฝรั่งราดหน้า

Ingredients

10 spears canned asparagus, cut into long pieces
3 seasoned shiitake mushrooms
5 rice-straw mushrooms, halved
5 disk-shaped slices of carrot
1 tbsp. wheat flour
1/2 tsp. sugar
1 tbsp. light soy sauce
1/2 cup water
2 tbsp. vegetable oil

Preparation

1. Heat 1 tablespoonful of the oil in a wok. When it is hot, put in the asparagus and stir fry until hot all the way through ; then, dip up onto a plate.
2. Pour the remaining oil into the wok, put in the two kinds of mushroom, the carrot, and the water and stir fry.
3. Season with the sugar and soy sauce. When everything is done, mix some water with the flour and add with stirring to thicken the sauce. Then, dip out over the asparagus.

Note : seasoned shiitake mushrooms (See page 20)

เครื่องปรุง

หน่อไม้ฝรั่งกระป๋อง หั่นท่อนยาว	10	ต้น
เห็ดหอมปรุงรส	3	ดอก
เห็ดฟางผ่าครึ่ง	5	ดอก
แครอทหั่นแว่น	5	ชิ้น
แป้งสาลี	1	ช้อนโต๊ะ
น้ำตาลทราย	1/2	ช้อนชา
ซีอิ๊วขาว	1	ช้อนโต๊ะ
น้ำ	1/2	ถ้วย
น้ำมันพืช	2	ช้อนโต๊ะ

วิธีทำ

1. ใส่น้ำมัน 1 ช้อนโต๊ะในกระทะ ตั้งไฟให้ร้อน ใส่หน่อไม้ฝรั่ง ผัดให้ร้อนทั่ว ตักขึ้นใส่จาน พักไว้
2. ใส่น้ำมันที่เหลือลงในกระทะ ใส่เห็ดหอม เห็ดฟาง แครอท น้ำ ผัดให้ทั่ว
3. ปรุงรสด้วยน้ำตาล ซีอิ๊วขาว ละลายแป้งสาลีกับน้ำใส่ ผัดสักครู่จนข้นดี ตักราดบนหน่อไม้ที่ใส่จานไว้

หมายเหตุ เห็ดหอมปรุงรส ดูสูตรเห็ดหอมปรุงรส หน้า 20

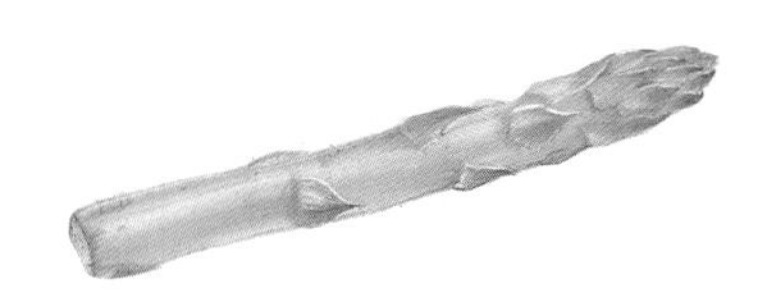

Phat Aetsaparakat Kap Het Hom

Stir-fried asparagus and shiitake mushrooms

ผัดแอสปารากัสกับเห็ดหอม

Ingredients

200 grams asparagus
5 shiitake mushrooms
3 crushed garlic cloves
2 tsp. tapioca flour
1/2 tbsp. light soy sauce
1 tbsp. oyster sauce
1/4 cup chicken stock
2 tbsp. cooking oil

Preparation

1. Remove the skin from the asparagus spears and wash. Scald the spears in boiling water, remove them immediately with a strainer and immerse in cold water, and then remove from the cold water and drain.
2. Soak dried shiitake mushrooms in water until softened, remove any tough portions of the stem, squeeze out excess water, and drain.
3. Heat the oil in a wok. When hot, fry the garlic until golden, and then add the mushrooms and stir fry. Add the stock, soy sauce, and oyster sauce, and then the asparagus. Mix the tapioca flour with a little water and add. Stir fry quickly over high heat ; then, remove from the heat.

เครื่องปรุง

แอสปารากัส	200	กรัม
เห็ดหอม	5	ดอก
กระเทียมทุบ	3	กลีบ
แป้งมัน	2	ช้อนชา
ซีอิ๊วขาว	1/2	ช้อนโต๊ะ
น้ำมันหอย	1	ช้อนโต๊ะ
น้ำซุป	1/4	ถ้วย
น้ำมัน	2	ช้อนโต๊ะ

วิธีทำ

1. ลอกผิวแอสปารากัสออก ล้างให้สะอาด หั่นเป็นท่อนสั้น นำไปลวกในน้ำเดือด ใช้กระชอนตักขึ้นนำไปแช่ในน้ำเย็นทันที แล้วตักขึ้นให้สะเด็ดน้ำ
2. แช่เห็ดหอมในน้ำจนนิ่ม ตัดเอาก้านดอกส่วนที่แข็ง ๆ ออก บีบน้ำผึ่งไว้
3. ใส่น้ำมันในกระทะ ตั้งไฟให้ร้อน เจียวกระเทียมพอเหลือง ใส่เห็ดหอมลงผัด ใส่น้ำซุปไก่ ซีอิ๊วขาว น้ำมันหอย ใส่แอสปารากัส ละลายแป้งมันในน้ำเล็กน้อยใส่ ผัดไฟแรงแล้วรีบปิดไฟยกลง

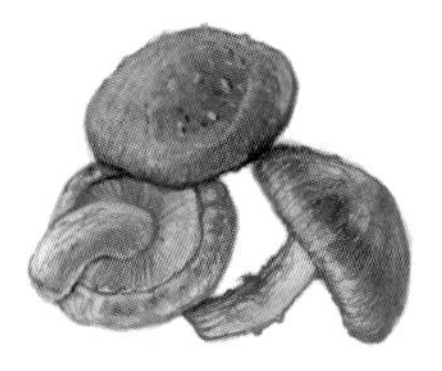

Dok Kui Chai Phat Pla Meuk

Stir-fried squid and Chinese chive flower stalks

ดอกกุยช่ายผัดปลาหมึก

Ingredients

300 grams Chinese chive flower stalks
200 grams squid
2 tsp. light soy sauce
2 tsp. oyster sauce
2 tsp. fish sauce
1/4 cup water
2 tbsp. cooking oil

Preparation

1. Remove any tough parts from the Chinese chive flower stalks, wash, and cut the stalks into 3-inch lengths.
2. Wash the squid, cut open, score the flesh in a criss-cross pattern, and then cut into large pieces.
3. Heat the oil in a wok. When hot, stir fry the Chinese chive flower stalks a few moments and then add the squid, water, fish sauce, soy sauce, and oyster sauce. Mix well, and when everything is done, turn off the heat and dip out onto a platter.

เครื่องปรุง

ดอกกุยช่าย	๓๐๐ กรัม
ปลาหมึกกล้วย	๒๐๐ กรัม
ซีอิ๊วขาว	๒ ช้อนชา
น้ำมันหอย	๒ ช้อนชา
น้ำปลา	๒ ช้อนชา
น้ำ	๑/๔ ถ้วย
น้ำมัน	๒ ช้อนโต๊ะ

วิธีทำ

1. ตัดส่วนแก่ของต้นกุยช่ายออก ล้างให้สะอาด หั่นยาว 3 นิ้ว
2. ล้างปลาหมึก กรีดด้านข้างตัวปลาหมึกให้แผ่ออก บั้งเป็นตาราง หั่นชิ้นใหญ่
3. ใส่น้ำมันในกระทะ ตั้งไฟให้ร้อน ใส่กุยช่าย ผัดสักครู่ ใส่ปลาหมึก น้ำ น้ำปลา ซีอิ๊วขาว น้ำมันหอย ผัดให้เข้ากัน สุกทั่วดีแล้วปิดไฟ ตักใส่จาน

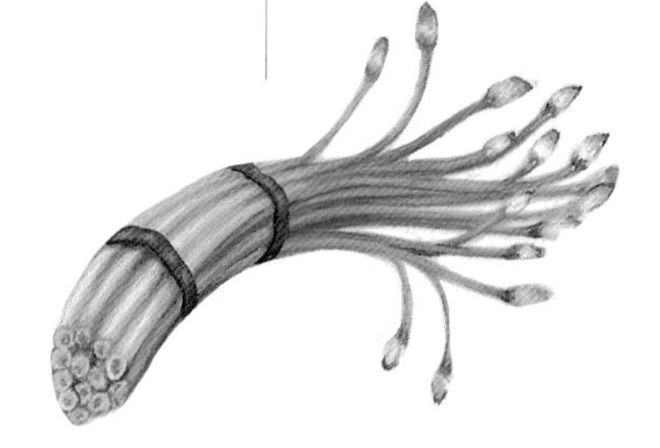

Pla Ka-phong Daeng Phat Kheun Chai

Stir-fried red snapper and celery

ปลากะพงแดงผัดขึ้นฉ่าย

Ingredients

1 cup chunks of red snapper meat
2 Chinese soup celery plants
2 garlic plants
2 red spur chillies
5 crushed garlic cloves
1 tbsp. sliced ginger
2 tbsp. light soy sauce
1 tbsp. salted bean
1/4 cup soup stock
3 tbsp. cooking oil

Preparation

1. Wash the garlic and celery plants ; cut the garlic into 2-inch lengths and the celery into 1-inch lengths.
2. Wash the spur chillies and slice lengthwise.
3. Heat the oil in a wok. When hot, add the garlic, salted bean, red snapper, and stock and stir fry.
4. Add light soy sauce to taste and continue frying a few moments.
5. Add the garlic plant, ginger, celery, and chilli, and when everything is done, remove from the heat.

เครื่องปรุง

เนื้อปลากะพงแดง		
หั่นสี่เหลี่ยม	1	ถ้วย
ขึ้นฉ่าย	2	ต้น
ต้นกระเทียม	2	ต้น
พริกชี้ฟ้าแดง	2	เม็ด
กระเทียมบุบ	5	กลีบ
ขิงซอย	1	ช้อนโต๊ะ
ซีอิ๊วขาว	2	ช้อนโต๊ะ
เต้าซี่	1	ช้อนโต๊ะ
น้ำซุป	1/4	ถ้วย
น้ำมัน	3	ช้อนโต๊ะ

วิธีทำ

1. ล้างต้นกระเทียมหั่นต้นยาว 2 นิ้ว ล้างขึ้นฉ่ายหั่นท่อนยาว 1 นิ้ว
2. ล้างพริกชี้ฟ้า หั่นตามยาว
3. ใส่น้ำมันลงในกระทะ ตั้งไฟให้ร้อน ใส่กระเทียม เต้าซี่ เนื้อปลา น้ำซุป
4. ปรุงรสด้วยซีอิ๊วขาว ผัดสักครู่
5. ใส่ต้นกระเทียม ขิง ขึ้นฉ่าย พริกชี้ฟ้า พอทุกอย่างสุกปิดไฟ

Kha-na Nam Man Hoi

Stir-fried kale and mushrooms

คะน้าน้ำมันหอย

Ingredients

300 grams tender young Chinese kale tips
200 grams rice-straw mushrooms
1 tbsp. finely sliced garlic
1 tsp. sugar
1 tbsp. light soy sauce
3 tbsp. oyster sauce
3 tbsp. chicken stock
2 tbsp. cooking oil

Preparation

1. Wash and drain the kale.
2. Heat the oil in a wok. When hot, add the garlic, fry until fragrant, add the kale and mushrooms and stir fry. Add the soy sauce, sugar, and stock. When the vegetables are done, add the oyster sauce, stir to mix thoroughly, dip out onto a platter, and serve.

Note : For crisp vegetables, fry just a short time; for more thoroughly cooked vegetables, fry longer.

เครื่องปรุง

ยอดคะน้าอ่อน	๓๐๐ กรัม
เห็ดฟาง	๒๐๐ กรัม
กระเทียมซอยบาง	๑ ช้อนโต๊ะ
น้ำตาลทราย	๑ ช้อนชา
ซีอิ๊วขาว	๑ ช้อนโต๊ะ
น้ำมันหอย	๓ ช้อนโต๊ะ
น้ำซุป	๓ ช้อนโต๊ะ
น้ำมัน	๒ ช้อนโต๊ะ

วิธีทำ

1. ล้างยอดคะน้าให้สะอาด พักไว้ให้สะเด็ดน้ำ
2. ใส่น้ำมันในกระทะ ตั้งไฟให้ร้อน ใส่กระเทียมเจียวให้หอม ใส่ยอดคะน้าและเห็ดฟาง ผัดให้ทั่ว ใส่ซีอิ๊วขาว น้ำตาล และน้ำซุป พอผักสุกใส่น้ำมันหอย ผัดให้ทั่ว ตักใส่จาน เสิร์ฟ

หมายเหตุ ถ้าชอบผักกรอบใช้เวลาผัดเร็ว ๆ ถ้าต้องการสุกมาก ผักนุ่มใช้เวลาเพิ่มขึ้น

Priao Wan

Sweet and sour stir-fried vegetables

เปรี้ยวหวาน

Ingredients

1/4 head red cabbage, sliced into bite-size pieces
2 cucumbers, cut lengthwise into slices
1 tomato, cut into wedges
2 bell chillies, cut lengthwise into large pieces
5-6 rice-straw mushrooms, sliced in half
1 cake white bean curd, cut in half, each half cut crosswise into thin slices
1 tbsp. wheat flour
1 tbsp. sugar
1/2 tbsp. tomato ketchup
2 tbsp. light soy sauce
1 tbsp. vinegar
1/2 cup water
2 tbsp. vegetable oil

Preparation

1. Heat the oil in a wok. When it is hot, put in the cabbage, cucumbers, tomato, bell chillies, mushrooms, bean curd, and water and stir fry. When everything is done, mix in the ketchup.
2. Season with the sugar, soy sauce, and vinegar. Mix some water with the flour and add with stirring to thicken. Taste and season additionally as desired, and then turn off the heat.

เครื่องปรุง

กะหล่ำปลีสีม่วง หั่นชิ้นพอคำ	1/4	หัว
แตงกวาหั่นสี่ตามยาว	2	ลูก
มะเขือเทศหั่นเสี้ยว	1	ลูก
พริกหยวกหั่นตามยาว ชิ้นใหญ่	2	เม็ด
เห็ดฟางผ่าครึ่ง	5-6	ดอก
เต้าหู้ขาวผ่าครึ่ง หั่นเป็นชิ้นบางตามขวาง	1	แผ่น
แป้งสาลี	1	ช้อนโต๊ะ
น้ำตาลทราย	1	ช้อนโต๊ะ
ซอสมะเขือเทศ	1/2	ช้อนโต๊ะ
ซีอิ๊วขาว	2	ช้อนโต๊ะ
น้ำส้มสายชู	1	ช้อนโต๊ะ
น้ำ	1/2	ถ้วย
น้ำมันพืช	2	ช้อนโต๊ะ

วิธีทำ

1. ใส่น้ำมันในกระทะ ตั้งไฟให้ร้อน ใส่กะหล่ำปลี แตงกวา มะเขือเทศ พริกหยวก เห็ดฟาง เต้าหู้ขาว ใส่น้ำ ผัดจนสุก ใส่ซอสมะเขือเทศ ผัดให้ทั่ว
2. ปรุงรสด้วยน้ำตาล ซีอิ๊วขาว น้ำส้มสายชู ละลายแป้งสาลีกับน้ำใส่ ผัดสักครู่ ชิมรส ปิดไฟ

Phak So-phon Rat Na

Leaf mustard with mushroom sauce

ผักโสภณราดหน้า

Ingredients

1 leaf mustard plant
100 grams rice-straw mushrooms, sliced in half
6 champignon mushrooms
1 tbsp. wheat flour
1/2 tsp. sugar
2 tbsp. light soy sauce
1/2 cup water
2 tbsp. vegetable oil

Preparation

1. Wash the mustard plant and cut into pieces. Immerse these in boiling water until tender. Remove from the water, drain, and then arrange on plate.
2. Heat the oil in a wok. When it is hot, put in both kinds of mushrooms and the water and stir fry.
3. Season with the sugar and soy sauce. Mix some water with the flour and add to the wok. Continue stir frying until the sauce is thick, and then dip out over the mustard.

เครื่องปรุง

ผักโสภณ	1	ต้น
เห็ดฟางผ่าครึ่ง	100	กรัม
เห็ดแชมปิญอง	6	ดอก
แป้งสาลี	1	ช้อนโต๊ะ
น้ำตาลทราย	1/2	ช้อนชา
ซีอิ๊วขาว	2	ช้อนโต๊ะ
น้ำ	1/2	ถ้วย
น้ำมันพืช	2	ช้อนโต๊ะ

วิธีทำ

1. ล้างผักโสภณ หั่นเป็นท่อน นำไปต้มในน้ำเดือดจนนิ่ม ตักขึ้น พักไว้ให้สะเด็ดน้ำใส่จานไว้
2. ใส่น้ำมันในกระทะ ตั้งไฟให้ร้อน ใส่เห็ดฟาง เห็ดแชมปิญอง น้ำ ผัดให้ทั่ว
3. ปรุงรสด้วยน้ำตาล ซีอิ๊วขาว ละลายแป้งสาลีกับน้ำใส่ ผัดสักครู่จนข้นดี ตักราดบนผักโสภณที่เตรียมไว้

Ma-Kheua Yao Phat Tao Jiao

Boiled eggplant with fermented soybean sauce

มะเขือยาวผัดเต้าเจี้ยว

Ingredients

1 long eggplant, cut into 4-inch lengths
5 rice-straw mushrooms, chopped coarsely
1 tbsp. fermented soybeans
2 red spur chillies, sliced lengthwise
1 cup sweet basil leaves
1 tsp. sugar
1 tbsp. light soy sauce
1 tbsp. vegetable oil

Preparation

1. Boil the eggplant in two cups of water to which has been added 1/2 teaspoonful of the sugar and 1/2 teaspoonful of the oil. When it is done, remove from the water.
2. Arrange on a plate, sprinkle with the basil leaves and chilli slices, and set aside.
3. Heat the oil in a wok. When it is hot, stir fry the mushrooms and fermented soybeans.
4. Season with the soy sauce and sugar, stir to mix thoroughly. When everything is done, dip out over the eggplant.

เครื่องปรุง

มะเขือยาวหั่นท่อนยาว 4 นิ้ว	1 ลูก
เห็ดฟางสับหยาบ	5 ดอก
เต้าเจี้ยว	1 ช้อนโต๊ะ
พริกชี้ฟ้าแดงหั่นตามยาว	2 เม็ด
โหระพาเด็ดเป็นใบ	1 ถ้วย
น้ำตาลทราย	1 ช้อนชา
ซีอิ๊วขาว	1 ช้อนโต๊ะ
น้ำมันพืช	1 ช้อนโต๊ะ

วิธีทำ

1. ต้มมะเขือยาวกับน้ำ 2 ถ้วย น้ำตาลทราย 1/2 ช้อนชา น้ำมันพืช 1/2 ช้อนชา พอสุกมะเขือนิ่ม ตักขึ้น
2. เรียงมะเขือใส่จาน โรยใบโหระพา พริกชี้ฟ้า พักไว้
3. ใส่น้ำมันในกระทะ ตั้งไฟให้ร้อน ใส่เห็ดฟาง เต้าเจี้ยว
4. ปรุงรสด้วยซีอิ๊วขาว น้ำตาล ผัดให้เข้ากัน ตัก ราดบนมะเขือยาว

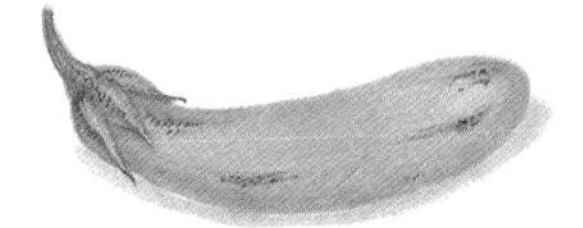

Ma-ra Phat Khai

Stir-fried bitter gourd and egg

มะระผัดไข่

Ingredients

1 Chinese bitter gourd
2 egg
1 tbsp. light soy sauce
1 tbsp. oyster sauce
2 tbsp. cooking oil

Preparation

1. Wash the bitter gourd, slice open lengthwise, remove and discard the insides, and cut into thin slices.
2. Heat the oil in a wok. When hot, stir fry the bitter gourd until tender, add soy sauce and oyster sauce, and stir to mix.
3. Break the egg into the wok, continue to stir fry until the egg is done, and then turn off the heat.

เครื่องปรุง

มะระจีน	๑ ลูก
ไข่	๒ ฟอง
ซีอิ๊วขาว	๑ ช้อนโต๊ะ
น้ำมันหอย	๑ ช้อนโต๊ะ
น้ำมัน	๒ ช้อนโต๊ะ

วิธีทำ

1. ล้างมะระผ่ากลางตามยาว ควักไส้ออก หั่นชิ้นบาง
2. ใส่น้ำมันในกระทะ ตั้งไฟให้ร้อน ใส่มะระ ผัดพอมะระนุ่ม ใส่ซีอิ๊วขาว น้ำมันหอย ผัดให้เข้ากัน
3. ต่อยไข่ใส่ ผัดพอไข่แห้ง ปิดไฟ

Phat Fak Sai Khai

Stir-fried wax gourd and egg

ผัดฟักใส่ไข่

Ingredients

1 wax gourd
2 eggs
1 tbsp. light soy sauce
1 tbsp. oyster sauce
1/2 tbsp. fish sauce
2 tbsp. cooking oil

Preparation

1. Wash and peel the gourd and cut into slices two inches long and half an inch thick.
2. Heat the oil in a wok. When hot, stir fry the gourd a short while and then add the soy sauce, fish sauce, and oyster sauce.
3. When the gourd is almost done, break the eggs into the wok, stir to mix everything, and then turn off the heat.

เครื่องปรุง

ฟัก	1 ลูก
ไข่	๒ ฟอง
ซีอิ๊วขาว	1 ช้อนโต๊ะ
น้ำมันหอย	1 ช้อนโต๊ะ
น้ำปลา	1/๒ ช้อนโต๊ะ
น้ำมัน	๒ ช้อนโต๊ะ

วิธีทำ

1. ล้างฟัก ปอกเปลือก หั่นเป็นชิ้นยาว 2 นิ้ว หนา 1/2 นิ้ว
2. ใส่น้ำมันในกระทะ ตั้งไฟให้ร้อน ใส่ฟักลงผัดสักครู่ ใส่ซีอิ๊วขาว น้ำปลา น้ำมันหอย
3. พอฟักจวนสุก ต่อยไข่ใส่ ผัดให้เข้ากัน ปิดไฟ

Fak Thong Phat Het

Stir-fried squash and mushrooms

ฟักทองผัดเห็ด

Ingredients

300 gram bite-size pieces of peeled squash
2 seasoned shiitake mushrooms, sliced
100 grams rice-straw mushrooms, cut into disk-shaped slices half a sheet of fried yuba, cut into bite-size pieces
1 Bhutanese oyster mushroom, torn into bite-size pieces
1/2 fried yuba sheet cut into bite-size
1 red spur chilli, sliced diagonally
1/2 cup horapha sweet basil leaves
1 tsp. sugar
2 tbsp. light soy sauce
1/4 cup water
2 vegetable oil

Preparation

1. Heat the oil in a wok. When it is hot, put in the squash and a little water and stir fry until it is done.
2. Season with the sugar and soy sauce and stir thoroughly.
3. Add the shiitake, rice-straw, and Bhutanese oyster mushrooms, the yuba, and the chilli and stir fry until everything is done.
4. Dip out onto a plate, sprinkle with basil leaves, and serve.

Note : seasoned shiitake mushrooms (See page 20)

เครื่องปรุง

ฟักทองปอกเปลือก หั่นชิ้นบางพอคำ	300	กรัม
เห็ดหอมปรุงรสหั่นเสี้ยว	2	ดอก
เห็ดฟางหั่นแว่น	100	กรัม
เห็ดนางฟ้าฉีกเป็นชิ้นพอคำ	1	ดอก
ฟองเต้าหู้ทอดหักเป็นชิ้นพอคำ	1/2	แผ่น
พริกชี้ฟ้าแดงหั่นเฉียง	1	เม็ด
โหระพาเด็ดเป็นใบ	1/2	ถ้วย
น้ำตาลทราย	1	ช้อนชา
ซีอิ๊วขาว	2	ช้อนโต๊ะ
น้ำ	1/4	ถ้วย
น้ำมันพืช	2	ช้อนโต๊ะ

วิธีทำ

1. ใส่น้ำมันในกระทะ ตั้งไฟให้ร้อน ใส่ฟักทอง เติมน้ำลงไปเล็กน้อย เพื่อให้ฟักทองนิ่ม ผัดจนสุก
2. ปรุงรสด้วยน้ำตาล ซีอิ๊วขาว ผัดให้ทั่ว
3. ใส่เห็ดหอม เห็ดฟาง เห็ดนางฟ้า ฟองเต้าหู้ พริกชี้ฟ้า ผัดให้สุก
4. ตักใส่จาน โรยใบโหระพา เสิร์ฟ

หมายเหตุ เห็ดหอมปรุงรส ดูสูตรเห็ดหอมปรุงรสหน้า 20

Het Phat Met Ma-muang Himaphan

Stir-Fried cashews and mushrooms

เห็ดผัดเม็ดมะม่วงหิมพานต์

Ingredients

100 grams rice-straw mushrooms, cut into thin slices
3 seasoned shiitake mushrooms, sliced
100 grams fried cashew nut
3 crisp-fried dried spur chillies
1 fresh red spur chilli, sliced lenghtwise
1 tsp. sugar
1/2 tsp. salt
1 tbsp. light soy sauce
1 tbsp. vegetable oil

Preparation

1. Heat the oil in a wok. When it is hot, put in the shiitake and rice-straw mushrooms, cashews, and fried chillies and stir fry.
2. Season with the sugar, salt, and soy sauce. When everything is ready, dip out onto a plate, sprinkle with the fresh chilli slices, and serve.

Note : seasoned shiitake mushrooms (See page 20)

เครื่องปรุง

เห็ดฟางหั่นชิ้นบาง	100	กรัม
เห็ดหอมปรุงรสหั่นเสี้ยว	3	ดอก
เม็ดมะม่วงหิมพานต์ทอด	100	กรัม
พริกชี้ฟ้าแห้งทอด	3	เม็ด
พริกชี้ฟ้าแดงหั่นตามยาว	1	เม็ด
น้ำตาลทราย	1	ช้อนชา
เกลือป่น	1/2	ช้อนชา
ซีอิ๊วขาว	1	ช้อนโต๊ะ
น้ำมันพืช	1	ช้อนโต๊ะ

วิธีทำ

1. ใส่น้ำมันในกระทะ ตั้งไฟให้ร้อน ใส่เห็ดฟาง เห็ดหอม เม็ดมะม่วงหิมพานต์ พริกทอด ผัดให้ทั่ว
2. ปรุงรสด้วยน้ำตาล เกลือ ซีอิ๊วขาว ผัดให้ทุกอย่างเข้ากัน ปิดไฟ ตักใส่จาน โรยพริกชี้ฟ้า เสิร์ฟ

หมายเหตุ เห็ดหอมปรุงรส ดูสูตรเห็ดหอมปรุงรส หน้า 20

Tao Hu Phat Kheun Chai

Stir-fried bean curd, mushrooms, and celery

เต้าหู้ผัดขึ้นฉ่าย

Ingredients

2 cakes soft yellow bean curd, cut into quarters
2 seasoned shiitake mushrooms, sliced
4 rice-straw mushrooms, cut into thin slices
4 Chinese soup celery plants, cut into 2-inch lengths
1/2 tsp. sugar
2 tbsp. light soy sauce
2 tbsp. water
2 tbsp. vegetable oil

Preparation

1. Heat the 2 tablespoonsful of oil in a clean wok. When it is hot, stir fry the two types of mushrooms. When they are about done, add the bean curd.
2. Season with the sugar and soy sauce, add the water, and when everything is done, put in the celery and turn off the heat.

Note : seasoned shiitake mushrooms (See page 20)

เครื่องปรุง

เต้าหู้เหลืองชนิดอ่อน หั่นเป็น 4 ชิ้นทอด	2	แผ่น
เห็ดหอมปรุงรสหั่นเสี้ยว	2	ดอก
เห็ดฟางหั่นแว่นบาง	4	ดอก
ขึ้นฉ่ายหั่นท่อนยาว 2 นิ้ว	4	ต้น
น้ำตาลทราย	1/2	ช้อนชา
ซีอิ๊วขาว	2	ช้อนโต๊ะ
น้ำ	2	ช้อนโต๊ะ
น้ำมันพืช	2	ช้อนโต๊ะ

วิธีทำ

1. ใส่น้ำมันในกระทะ ตั้งไฟให้ร้อน ใส่เห็ดฟาง เห็ดหอม ผัดให้ทั่ว พอสุก ใส่เต้าหู้
2. ปรุงรสด้วยน้ำตาล ซีอิ๊วขาว ใส่น้ำ ผัดให้สุกทั่วกันดี ใส่ขึ้นฉ่าย ปิดไฟ

หมายเหตุ เห็ดหอมปรุงรส ดูสูตรเห็ดหอมปรุงรส หน้า 20

Tao Hu Song Khreuang

Steamed bean curd with mushroom sauce

เต้าหู้ทรงเครื่อง

Ingredients

2 tubes soft bean curd
3 seasoned shiitake mushrooms, cut into small pieces
7 rice-straw mushrooms, cut in half
1 Chinese soup celery plant, cut into 2-inch lengths
1 tbsp. wheat flour
1/2 tsp. sugar
2 tbsp. light soy sauce
1/2 cup water
1 tbsp. vegetable oil for cooking

Preparation

1. Cut the bean curd into 2-inch-long cylinders, steam them for 15 minutes, arrange them on a plate, and set aside.
2. Heat the oil in a wok. When it is hot, put in the two kinds of mushrooms, and the water and stir fry.
3. Season with the sugar and soy sauce. When about ready, mix some water with the flour and add with stirring to thicken. Then, add the celery, and dip out over the steamed bean curd.

Note : seasoned shiitake mushrooms (See page 20)

เครื่องปรุง

เต้าหู้หลอด	๒	หลอด
เห็ดหอมปรุงรสหั่นชิ้นเล็ก	๓	ดอก
เห็ดฟางผ่าครึ่ง	๗	ดอก
ขึ้นฉ่ายหั่นยาว ๒ นิ้ว	๑	ต้น
แป้งสาลี	๑	ช้อนโต๊ะ
น้ำตาลทราย	๑/๒	ช้อนชา
ซีอิ๊วขาว	๒	ช้อนโต๊ะ
น้ำ	๑/๒	ถ้วย
น้ำมันพืช	๑	ช้อนโต๊ะ

วิธีทำ

1. หั่นเต้าหู้เป็นท่อนยาว 2 นิ้ว นำไปนึ่งประมาณ 15 นาที ใส่จาน พักไว้
2. ใส่น้ำมันในกระทะ ตั้งไฟให้ร้อน ใส่เห็ดหอม เห็ดฟาง น้ำ ผัดให้ทั่ว
3. ปรุงรสด้วยน้ำตาล ซีอิ๊วขาว ละลายแป้งสาลีกับน้ำใส่ ผัดสักครู่ ใส่ขึ้นฉ่าย ตักราดบนเต้าหู้ที่เตรียมไว้

หมายเหตุ เห็ดหอมปรุงรส ดูสูตรเห็ดหอมปรุงรส หน้า 20

Sup Phak Suk

Cooked vegetable soup

ซุปผักสุก

Ingredients

1 Chinese radish
1 young garlic plant
1/2 cup boiled green beans cut into 1-cm lengths
1/2 cup boiled carrot cut into disks
1/2 cup boiled caulifiawere, cut into small pieces
1 Chinese soup celery plant
neck and back of one chicken, cut into large pieces
2 tsp. salt
6 cups water
sprigs of parsley

Preparation

1. Pour the water into a pot and put the chicken bones in. Wash the celery, cut off the root, tie the stems in a knot, and put them into the pot. Put in the garlic plant. Peel the radish, cut it into large pieces, and put these in the pot. Place the pot on low heat and simmer slowly for about an hour. Remove the vegetables, filter the broth through a fine-meshed white cloth into a pot, and then heat to bring the broth to a boil.
2. Put in the beans, carrot, and cauliflower, continue heating for a short time, season with the salt, dip into bowl and garnish with the parsley.

เครื่องปรุง

หัวผักกาดขาว 1 หัว
ต้นกระเทียม 1 ต้น
ถั่วแขกต้มหั่นท่อน 1 ซม. 1/2 ถ้วย
แครอทต้มสุกหั่นแว่น 1/2 ซม. 1/2 ถ้วย
ดอกกะหล่ำต้มหั่นเป็นชิ้นเล็ก 1/2 ถ้วย
ขึ้นฉ่าย 1 ต้น
กระดูกไก่สับเป็นชิ้นใหญ่ ๆ 1 ตัว
เกลือป่น 2 ช้อนชา
น้ำ 6 ถ้วย
Parsley สำหรับแต่งหน้า

วิธีทำ

1. ใส่น้ำและกระดูกไก่ลงในหม้อ ล้างขึ้นฉ่ายตัดรากออกผูกเป็นกำใส่ลงในหม้อพร้อมกับต้นกระเทียมและหัวผักกาดขาวปอกเปลือกหั่นท่อนใหญ่ ๆ ใส่ลงในหม้อ ตั้งไฟอ่อน เคี่ยวประมาณ 1 ชั่วโมง ตักผักออกกรองด้วยผ้าขาวบาง ใส่ลงในหม้อ ตั้งต่อพอเดือด
2. ใส่ถั่วแขก แครอท ดอกกะหล่ำ ลงในหม้อน้ำซุป ตั้งไฟต่อสักครู่ ปรุงรสด้วยเกลือ พอร้อนตักใส่ถ้วยซุป แต่งด้วย Parsley

Sup Sa-khu

Tapioca and egg soup

ซุปสาคู

Ingredients

1/4 cup tapioca pellets
1 hen's egg, beaten
1/2 tsp. ground pepper
1 tsp. salt
1 tsp. sherry
3 1/2 cups chicken stock
a few sprigs of parsley

Preparation

1. Wash the tapioca pellets to remove any dust or foreign matter.
2. Filter the stock through cheese-cloth into a pot, bring it to a boil, add the tapioca, and stir well.
3. Season with the salt and pepper. Add the egg by pouring it into a colander gently moved to and fro over the pot so that thin streams of egg flow into the soup. When the egg is done, add the sherry, remove from the heat, transfer to a bowl, and garnish with the parsley. You may wish to serve crackers with this soup.

เครื่องปรุง

สาคู	**1/4 ถ้วย**
ไข่ตีเข้ากัน	**1 ฟอง**
พริกไทยป่น	**1/2 ช้อนชา**
เกลือป่น	**1 ช้อนชา**
เหล้าเชอร์รี่	**1 ช้อนชา**
น้ำซุปไก่	**3 1/2 ถ้วย**
Parsley สำหรับแต่งหน้า	

วิธีทำ

1. ล้างสาคู กรองเอาเศษผงออก
2. กรองน้ำซุปไก่ให้ใส ใส่หม้อตั้งไฟพอเดือด ใส่สาคู คนพอทั่ว
3. ปรุงรสด้วยเกลือ พริกไทย เทไข่ใส่ในกระชอน วางเหนือหม้อ ส่ายกระชอนไปมาให้ไข่ไหลลงในหม้อเป็นสายเล็ก ๆ พอไข่สุกใส่เหล้าเชอร์รี่ ยกลงแต่งหน้าด้วย Parsley เสิร์ฟกับขนมปัง-กรอบประเภทแครกเกอร์ก็ได้

Sup Luk Deuei

Pearl barley soup

ซุปลูกเดือย

Ingredients

1/2 cup boiled pearl barley
2 tbsp. coarsely chopped chinese soup celery
3 tbsp. coarsely chopped onion
3 tbsp. coarsely chopped Chinese radish
2 tbsp. wheat flour
1/2 tsp. ground pepper
1 tsp. salt
3 1/2 cups beef stock
2 tbsp. butter
a few sprigs of parsley

Preparation

1. Stir fry the celery, onion, and radish using the butter. When the vegetables are done, dip them out of the wok and set them aside.
2. Stir the flour into the butter remaining in the wok and continue cooking until fragrant.
3. Pour the stock into a pot, put in the vegetables, the contents of the wok, and the boiled pearl barley, place the pot on low heat, and simmer until the vegetables are tender, seasoning with salt and pepper.
4. Transfer to a bowl, garnish with the parsley, and serve with crackers.

เครื่องปรุง

ลูกเดือยต้ม	1/2	ถ้วย
ขึ้นฉ่ายสับหยาบ ๆ	2	ช้อนโต๊ะ
หอมใหญ่สับหยาบ ๆ	3	ช้อนโต๊ะ
หัวผักกาดขาวสับหยาบ ๆ	3	ช้อนโต๊ะ
แป้งสาลี	2	ช้อนโต๊ะ
พริกไทยป่น	1/2	ช้อนชา
เกลือป่น	1	ช้อนชา
น้ำซุป	3 1/2	ถ้วย
เนย	2	ช้อนโต๊ะ

Parsley สำหรับแต่งหน้า

วิธีทำ

1. ผัดขึ้นฉ่าย หอมใหญ่ หัวผักกาดขาวกับเนย พอสุกยกลง ตักผักออกพักไว้
2. ผัดแป้งสาลีกับน้ำมันที่เหลือสักครู่ พอมีกลิ่นหอมยกลง
3. ใส่น้ำซุปในหม้อ ใส่ผัก แป้งสาลีที่ผัดแล้วและลูกเดือยต้มลงในหม้อ ตั้งไฟอ่อน เคี่ยวไปจนผักนุ่ม ปรุงด้วยเกลือ พริกไทย
4. ตักใส่ถ้วยซุป แต่งหน้าด้วย Parsley เสิร์ฟกับขนมปังแครกเกอร์

Ma-ra Tom Kra-duk Mu

Bitter gourd boiled with pork bones

มะระต้มกระดูกหมู

Ingredients

1 Chinese bitter gourd
200 grams meaty pork bones
1 tsp. chopped coriander greens
2 tbsp. fish sauce
2 cups water

Preparation

1. Wash the gourd, cut in half length wise, remove and discard the seeds, and cut the flesh into 1" × 2" pieces.
2. Boil the bones in the water, skimming off the scum as it forms. After a while, add the bitter gourd and fish sauce, and put the lid on the pot. Do not stir. Continue cooking until the gourd is well done, and then turn off the heat.
3. Sprinkle with the coriander greens and serve hot.

เครื่องปรุง

มะระจีนยาว	๑ ลูก
กระดูกหมู	๒๐๐ กรัม
ผักชีซอย	๑ ช้อนชา
น้ำปลา	๒ ช้อนโต๊ะ
น้ำ	๒ ถ้วย

วิธีทำ

1. ล้างมะระให้สะอาด ผ่าครึ่งตามยาว เอาไส้ทิ้ง หั่นเป็นชิ้น 1×2 นิ้ว
2. ต้มกระดูกหมูกับน้ำ หมั่นช้อนฟองทิ้ง สักครู่ ใส่มะระ ใส่น้ำปลา ปิดฝา อย่าคน ทิ้งไว้จน มะระสุกเปื่อย ปิดไฟ
3. โรยหน้าด้วยผักชี เสิร์ฟร้อน ๆ

No Mai Kra-pong Tom Phakkat Khao

Boiled asparagus and Chinese cabbage

หน่อไม้กระป๋องต้มผักกาดขาว

Ingredients

5 spears canned asparagus, cut into short lengths
3 seasoned shiitake mushrooms, sliced
100 grams rice-straw mushrooms, cut in half
1 head Chinese cabbage, separated into individual leaves
2 tbsp. light soy sauce
1 1/2 cups water

Preparation

1. Pour the water into a pot, bring to a boil, and put in the two kinds of mushrooms and the asparagus.
2. Season with the soy sauce. When everything is done, put in the cabbage leaves and turn off the heat.

Note : seasoned shiitake mushrooms (See page 20)

เครื่องปรุง

หน่อไม้ฝรั่งกระป๋อง หั่นท่อนสั้น	5	ต้น
เห็ดหอมปรุงรสหั่นเสี้ยว	3	ดอก
เห็ดฟางผ่าครึ่ง	100	กรัม
ผักกาดขาวเด็ดเป็นใบ	1	ต้น
ซีอิ๊วขาว	2	ช้อนโต๊ะ
น้ำ	1 1/2	ถ้วย

วิธีทำ

1. ใส่น้ำลงในหม้อ ตั้งไฟให้เดือด ใส่เห็ดหอม เห็ดฟาง หน่อไม้ฝรั่ง
2. ปรุงรสด้วยซีอิ๊วขาว พอสุกทั่วใส่ผักกาดขาว ปิดไฟ

หมายเหตุ เห็ดหอมปรุงรส ดูสูตรเห็ดหอมปรุงรสหน้า 20

Kaeng Jeut Phak Chi

Pork and coriander soup

แกงจืดผักชี

Ingredients

100 grams coriander plants
200 grams pork
1 tbsp. light soy sauce
1/2 tsp. salt
2 cups water

Preparation

1. Wash and clean the coriander plants and then chop, roots and all, with the pork.
2. Mix the soy sauce and salt with the chopped pork and coriander.
3. Bring the water to a boil in a pot. Form the chopped pork and coriander into lumps and drop into the water. When the meat is done, taste and season as desired ; then, turn off the heat and serve hot.

เครื่องปรุง

ผักชี	๑๐๐ กรัม
เนื้อหมู	๒๐๐ กรัม
ซีอิ๊วขาว	๑ ช้อนโต๊ะ
เกลือป่น	๑/๒ ช้อนชา
น้ำ	๒ ถ้วย

วิธีทำ

1. ล้างผักชีให้สะอาด แล้วสับกับเนื้อหมู โดยสับผักชีทั้งราก
2. ใส่ซีอิ๊วขาว และเกลือ เคล้าให้เข้ากับผักชีและหมูสับ
3. เอาน้ำใส่หม้อตั้งไฟ ปั้นหมูสับกับผักชีใส่ พอสุกชิมรสตามชอบ ปิดไฟ เสิร์ฟร้อน ๆ

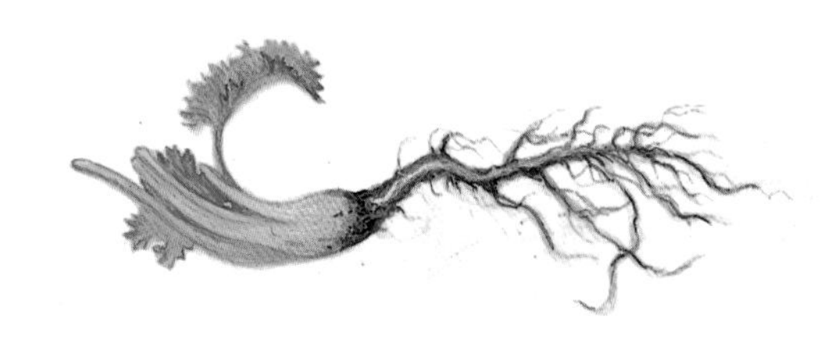

Kaeng Jeut Mu Sap Kap Khai

Ground pork and egg in soup

แกงจืดหมูสับกับไข่

Ingredients

100 grams chopped pork
1 egg
100 grams fresh ear mushrooms
1/2 tsp. dried salted vegetable
1 tsp. coriander leaves
2 tsp. salt
1 tbsp. light soy sauce
1 tbsp. fish sauce
2 cups water

Preparation

1. Rub the mushrooms with the salt and a little water, wash in fresh water, and then place them in a colander to drain.
2. Break the egg into a bowl containing the pork, beat them together, add the soy sauce, form into lumps.
3. Heat the water in a pot, and when it boils, put in the pork already prepared. When the soup returns to a boil, add the mushrooms, season to taste with fish sauce, turn off the heat, and sprinkle the soup with the dried salted vegetable and coriander greens.

เครื่องปรุง

หมูสับ	๑๐๐ กรัม
ไข่	๑ ฟอง
เห็ดหูหนูสด	๑๐๐ กรัม
ตังฉ่าย	๑/๒ ช้อนชา
ผักชีเด็ดเป็นใบ	๑ ช้อนโต๊ะ
เกลือป่น	๒ ช้อนชา
ซีอิ๊วขาว	๑ ช้อนโต๊ะ
น้ำปลา	๑ ช้อนโต๊ะ
น้ำ	๒ ถ้วย

วิธีทำ

1. ล้างเห็ดหูหนู โดยซาวกับเกลือแล้วล้างน้ำ 1 ครั้ง ใส่กระชอนพักไว้
2. ต่อยไข่ใส่ชามหมูสับ ตีให้เข้ากัน ใส่ซีอิ๊วขาว
3. เอาน้ำใส่หม้อตั้งไฟ พอเดือดตักหมูใส่ให้เป็นก้อน เดือดอีกครั้ง ใส่เห็ดหูหนู น้ำปลา ชิมรสตามชอบ ปิดไฟ โรยตังฉ่าย ผักชี

Tom Jeut Hua Phakkat Khao Song Khreuang

Radish soup

ต้มจืดหัวผักกาดขาวทรงเครื่อง

Ingredients

2 Chinese radishes
200 grams meaty pork bones
1 medium-sized dried squid
10 large dried shrimp
2 tbsp. fish sauce
2 cup water

Preparation

1. Peel the radishes, cut them into 3-inch lengths, and then cut each of these into quarters.
2. Wash the bones and the squid. Cut the squid crosswise into slices 1/2-inch wide.
3. Bring the water to a boil, put in the bones, reduce the heat, and simmer slowly, skimming off scum regularly to keep the soup clear.
4. After a short while, add the radish, squid, shrimp, and fish sauce, simmer until the radish is tender, and then turn off the heat.

เครื่องปรุง

หัวผักกาดขาว	๒	หัว
กระดูกหมู	๒๐๐	กรัม
ปลาหมึกแห้งขนาดกลาง	๑	ตัว
กุ้งแห้งตัวใหญ่	๑๐	ตัว
น้ำปลา	๒	ช้อนโต๊ะ
น้ำ	๒	ถ้วย

วิธีทำ

1. ปอกเปลือกหัวผักกาดขาว หั่นเป็นท่อนยาว 3 นิ้ว แล้วผ่าแบ่งเป็นสี่ชิ้น
2. ล้างกระดูกหมู ล้างปลาหมึก หั่นขวางลำตัวหนา 1 ซม.
3. เอาน้ำใส่หม้อตั้งไฟ พอเดือดใส่กระดูกหมู ลดไฟให้เดือดเพียงเบา ๆ หมั่นช้อนฟองทิ้งเพื่อให้น้ำใส
4. สักครู่ใส่หัวผักกาดขาว ปลาหมึก กุ้งแห้ง และน้ำปลา ต้มไปจนหัวผักกาดขาวเปื่อย ปิดไฟ

Pla Paen Tom Tao Jiao

Pony fish boiled with fermented soybeans

ปลาแป้นต้มเต้าเจี้ยว

Ingredients

2 pony fish
2 tbsp. fermented soybeans
1 tbsp. shredded ginger
1/2 cup coriander leaves
1 tbsp. light soy sauce
2 cups water
2 tsp. cooking oil

Preparation

1. Wash the ginger, scrub with salt, rinse off the salt, and soak the ginger in fresh water.
2. Clean and wash the fish.
3. Heat the water in a pot. When it boils, put in the fermented soybeans, ginger, and soy sauce, and then the fish and the oil. Put the lid on the pot, and boil for 10 to 15 minutes, until done. Turn off the heat, then dip up onto a bowl. Sprinkle with the coriander leaves and serve.

เครื่องปรุง

ปลาแป้น	๒ ตัว
เต้าเจี้ยว	๒ ช้อนโต๊ะ
ขิงซอย	๑ ช้อนโต๊ะ
ผักชีเด็ดเป็นใบ	๑/๒ ถ้วย
ซีอิ๊วขาว	๑ ช้อนโต๊ะ
น้ำ	๒ ถ้วย
น้ำมัน	๒ ช้อนชา

วิธีทำ

1. ล้างขิง ซาวกับเกลือแล้วล้างน้ำทิ้ง แช่ขิงไว้
2. ควักไส้ปลาทิ้ง ล้างปลาให้สะอาด
3. เอาน้ำใส่หม้อตั้งไฟ พอเดือดใส่เต้าเจี้ยว ขิง ซีอิ๊วขาว แล้วใส่ปลา ใส่น้ำมัน ปิดฝา ตั้งไฟสักครู่กะว่าปลาสุก (ประมาณ 10-15 นาที) ปิดไฟ ตักใส่ถ้วย โรยผักชี เสิร์ฟ

Kalampli Tun Het Hom

Cabbage stewed with shiitake mushrooms

กะหล่ำปลีตุ๋นเห็ดหอม

Ingredients

1 head cabbage, cut into quarters
4 seasoned shiitake mushrooms
1 Chinese soup celery plant, cut into 2-inch lengths
1/2 tsp. sugar
2 tbsp. light soy sauce
1 tsp. sweet dark soy sauce
2 cups water
1 cup vegetable oil for frying

Preparation

1. Heat the oil in a wok. When hot, fry the cabbage for a while and then remove and allow to stand.
2. Place the cabbage and mushrooms in a pot.
3. Mix together the light and dark soy sauces, the sugar, and the water, stir until the sugar dissolves, and then spoon over the cabbage in the pot. Place the lid on the pot and simmer slowly for about half an hour.
4. Dip out onto the serving bowl, sprinkle with celery and serve.

Note : seasoned shiitake mushrooms (See page 20)

เครื่องปรุง

กะหล่ำปลีผ่าเป็นสี่ส่วน	1	หัว
เห็ดหอมปรุงรส	4	ดอก
ขึ้นฉ่ายหั่นยาว ๒ นิ้ว	1	ต้น
น้ำตาลทราย	1/๒	ช้อนชา
ซีอิ๊วขาว	๒	ช้อนโต๊ะ
ซีอิ๊วดำ	1	ช้อนชา
น้ำ	๒	ถ้วย
น้ำมันพืช	1	ถ้วย

วิธีทำ

1. ใส่น้ำมันในกระทะ ตั้งไฟให้ร้อน ใส่กะหล่ำปลีทอดสักครู่ ตักขึ้น พักไว้
2. วางกะหล่ำปลีในถ้วยตุ๋น ใส่เห็ดหอม
3. ผสมซีอิ๊วขาว ซีอิ๊วดำ น้ำตาล น้ำ คนให้ส่วนผสมละลายเข้ากันดี ตักราดบนกะหล่ำปลี นำไปตุ๋น ประมาณ 30 นาที
4. ตักใส่ถ้วย โรยขึ้นฉ่าย เสิร์ฟ

หมายเหตุ เห็ดหอมปรุงรส ดูสูตรเห็ดหอมปรุงรส หน้า 20

Tom Yam Het Sot

Sour and spicy mushroom soup

ต้มยำเห็ดสด

Ingredients

7 rice-straw mushrooms, cut in half
5 Bhutanese oyster mushrooms, torn into bite-size pieces
2 seasoned shiitake mushrooms
1 Chinese soup celery plant, cut into 2-inch lengths
5 hot chillies, sliced in half lengthwise
3 disk-shapped slices of galangal
2 lemon grass stems, cut diagonally into 2-inch lengths
2 kaffir lime leaves
1/2 tsp. sugar
2 tbsp. light soy sauce
2 tbsp. lime juice
1 cup water

Preparation

1. Pour the water into a pot, put in the galangal, lemon grass, kaffir lime leaves, and chillies, and place on the heat.
2. When the water boils, add the three kinds of mushrooms.
3. Season with the sugar and soy sauce, and when everything is done, add the celery, turn off the heat, and add the lime juice.

Taste additionally if desired, serve.

Note : seasoned shiitake mushrooms (See page 20)

เครื่องปรุง

เห็ดฟางผ่าครึ่ง	๗	ดอก
เห็ดนางฟ้าฉีกเป็นชิ้นพอคำ	๕	ดอก
เห็ดหอมปรุงรส	๒	ดอก
ขึ้นฉ่ายหั่นยาว ๒ นิ้ว	๑	ต้น
พริกขี้หนูหั่นตามยาว	๕	เม็ด
ข่า	๓	แว่น
ตะไคร้หั่นเฉียงยาว ๒ นิ้ว	๒	ต้น
ใบมะกรูด	๒	ใบ
น้ำตาลทราย	๑/๒	ช้อนชา
ซีอิ๊วขาว	๒	ช้อนโต๊ะ
น้ำมะนาว	๒	ช้อนโต๊ะ
น้ำ	๑	ถ้วย

วิธีทำ

1. ใส่น้ำลงในหม้อ ใส่ข่า ตะไคร้ ใบมะกรูด พริกขี้หนู ตั้งไฟพอเดือด
2. ใส่เห็ดฟาง เห็ดนางฟ้า เห็ดหอม
3. ปรุงรสด้วยน้ำตาล ซีอิ๊วขาว พอสุกทั่วใส่ขึ้นฉ่าย ปิดไฟ ใส่น้ำมะนาว ชิมรส เสิร์ฟ

หมายเหตุ เห็ดหอมปรุงรส ดูสูตรเห็ดหอมปรุงรส หน้า 20

Khao Kung Phrik Khi Nu

Rice fried with prawns and hot chillies

ข้าวกุ้งพริกขี้หนู

Ingredients

2 cups cooked rice
200 grams white or tiger prawns
2 tbsp. crushed green and red hot chillies
1/2 cup onion sliced lengthwise
1 tbsp. chopped garlic
1 tbsp. sugar
2 tbsp. fish sauce
1/4 cup cooking oil

Preparation

1. Wash and shell the prawns, leaving the tail fins in place. Cut open down the back and remove the dark vein.
2. Pour the oil into a wok and place on medium heat. When it is hot, put in the garlic and fry until golden ; then, add the prawns, chillies, and onion.
3. Season with the sugar and fish sauce, and continue stir frying until the prawns are done and fragrant.
4. Now, add the rice and stir fry with the prawns. Serve hot with cucumber and spring onion.

เครื่องปรุง

ข้าวสวย	๒	ถ้วย
กุ้งชีแฮ้หรือกุ้งกุลาดำ	๒๐๐	กรัม
พริกขี้หนูเขียวแดงบุบ	๒	ช้อนโต๊ะ
หอมใหญ่หั่นยาว	๑/๒	ถ้วย
กระเทียมสับ	๑	ช้อนโต๊ะ
น้ำตาลทราย	๑	ช้อนโต๊ะ
น้ำปลา	๒	ช้อนโต๊ะ
น้ำมัน	๑/๔	ถ้วย

วิธีทำ

1. ล้างกุ้ง ปอกเปลือกไว้หาง ผ่าหลังชักเส้นดำ
2. ใส่น้ำมันในกระทะ ตั้งไฟกลาง พอร้อนใส่กระเทียม เจียวพอเหลือง ใส่กุ้ง พริกขี้หนู หอมใหญ่
3. ปรุงรสด้วยน้ำตาล น้ำปลา ผัดจนกุ้งสุกหอม
4. ใส่ข้าว ผัดกับกุ้งให้เข้ากัน พอสุกทั่ว ตักใส่จาน เสิร์ฟร้อน ๆ กับแตงกวา ต้นหอม

Khao Phat Sai-krok Salami kap Phak

Rice with vegetable sauce and salami

ข้าวผัดไส้กรอกซาลามี่กับผัก

Ingredients

1 cup milled rice
200 grams long thin slices of salami
1/2 cup boiled corn kernels
3 tbsp. small pieces of green pepper
3 tbsp. rasins
1/4 tsp. ground pepper
1/2 tsp. sugar
1 tsp. salt
1/2 tsp. powdered mustard
1 tsp. red wine
1 1/2 cups water
1/4 cup cooking oil

Preparation

1. Cook the rice with the salt.
2. Mix the mustard, wine, sugar, pepper, and oil in a wok and heat. When everything is mixed well, add the rasins, green pepper, and corn, stir well, and remove from the heat. Add the rice and mix everything together.
3. Dip onto a plate and serve with the salami. Sprinkle with parsley.

เครื่องปรุง

ข้าวสาร	1	ถ้วย
ไส้กรอกซาลามี่หั่นเป็นริ้ว ๆ หนา 1/2 ซ.ม.	200	กรัม
ข้าวโพดต้มแกะเมล็ด	1/2	ถ้วย
พริกหวานหั่นเป็นชิ้นเล็ก ๆ	3	ช้อนโต๊ะ
ลูกเกด	3	ช้อนโต๊ะ
พริกไทยป่น	1/4	ช้อนชา
น้ำตาลทราย	1/2	ช้อนชา
เกลือ	1	ช้อนชา
ผงมัสตาร์ด	1/2	ช้อนชา
ไวน์แดง	1	ช้อนชา
น้ำ	1 1/2	ถ้วย
น้ำมัน	1/4	ถ้วย

วิธีทำ

1. หุงข้าวใส่เกลือ
2. ผสมมัสตาร์ด ไวน์แดง น้ำตาล พริกไทย และน้ำมัน ใส่ในกระทะยกขึ้นตั้งไฟพอเครื่องเข้ากันดีใส่ลูกเกด พริกหวาน ข้าวโพด คนให้ทั่ว ยกลงนำมาคลุกกับข้าว เคล้าให้เข้ากัน
3. ตักใส่จาน รับประทานกับไส้กรอกซาลามี่ แต่งหน้าด้วย Parsley

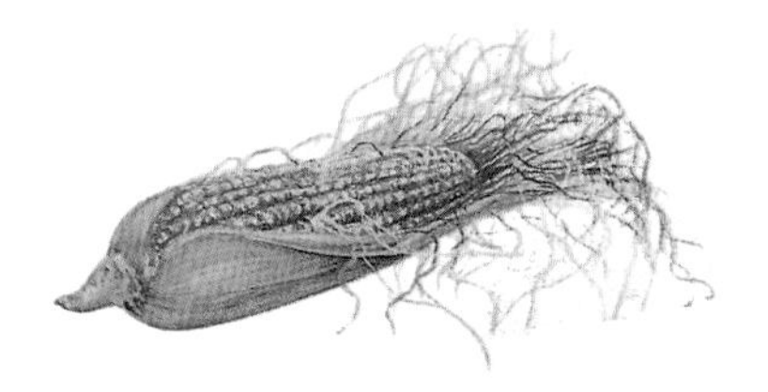

Khao Phat Met Ma-muang Himaphan

Fried rice with cashews

ข้าวผัดเม็ดมะม่วงหิมพานต์

Ingredients

1 cup cooked rice
2 tbsp. fried cashews nut
2 tbsp. small pieces of carrot
2 shiitake mushrooms, soaked in water and cut into small pieces
5 crushed garlic cloves
1 tsp. sugar
1 tbsp. light soy sauce
1/2-1 tbsp. fish sauce
3 tbsp. cooking oil

Preparation

1. Heat the oil in a wok. When it is hot, fry the garlic until fragrant, and then add the carrot and mushroom. When they are done, add the rice and stir fry.
2. Season with the sugar and soy sauce and fish sauces and continue stir frying. When ready, dip up onto a plate and sprinkle with the cashews, and serve.

เครื่องปรุง

ข้าวสวย	๑	ถ้วย
เม็ดมะม่วงหิมพานต์ทอด	๒	ช้อนโต๊ะ
แครอทหั่นสี่เหลี่ยมลูกเต๋า	๒	ช้อนโต๊ะ
เห็ดหอมแช่น้ำให้นุ่ม หั่นชิ้นเล็ก	๒	ดอก
กระเทียมบุบ	๕	กลีบ
น้ำตาลทราย	๑	ช้อนชา
ซีอิ๊วขาว	๑	ช้อนโต๊ะ
น้ำปลา	๒	ช้อนโต๊ะ
น้ำมัน	๓	ช้อนโต๊ะ

วิธีทำ

1. ใส่น้ำมันในกระทะ ตั้งไฟให้ร้อน ใส่กระเทียมเจียวให้หอม ใส่แครอทและเห็ดหอม ผัดให้สุก ใส่ข้าว ผัดให้เข้ากัน
2. ปรุงรสด้วยน้ำตาล ซีอิ๊วขาว น้ำปลา ผัดให้ทั่ว ตักใส่จาน โรยหน้าด้วยเม็ดมะม่วงหิมพานต์ เสิร์ฟ

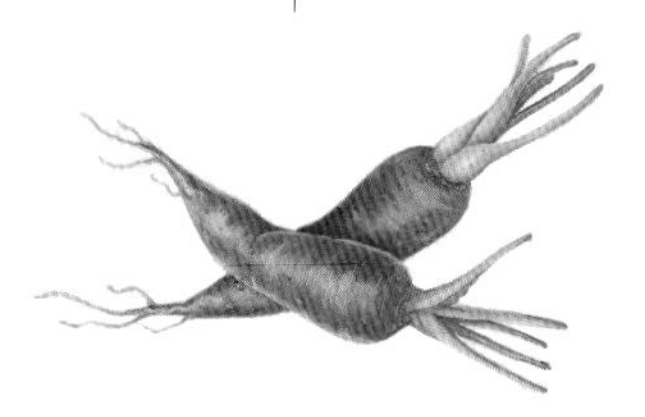

Khao Phat Ham Ka-phrao Krop

Ham and holy basil fried rice

ข้าวผัดแฮมกะเพรากรอบ

Ingredients

1 cup cooked rice
1/2 cup bite-size slices of cooked ham
1 tbsp. pounded green and red spur chillies
1/2 tsp. chopped hot chillies
1 tbsp. chopped garlic
4 cups holy basil leaves
1/2 tsp. ground pepper
1 tbsp. sugar
1 tbsp. light soy sauce
1 tbsp. fish sauce
1/4 cup cooking oil

Preparation

1. Pour the oil into a wok over high heat. When it is hot, turn down the heat, fry about two cups of the basil leaves quickly, and then remove them from the oil and put them on absorbent paper to drain.
2. Place the oil in which the basil leaves were fried on medium heat. When hot, put in the garlic, hot and spur chillies, and pepper, fry until fragrant, and then add the ham and stir fry.
3. Season with the sugar, soy sauce, and fish sauce. Add the remaining basil leaves, and when they are done, put in the rice, and stir fry until it is ready.
4. Dip up the fried rice onto a plate, sprinkle on the fried basil leaves.

เครื่องปรุง

ข้าวสวย	1	ถ้วย
แฮมหั่นชิ้นพอคำ	1/2	ถ้วย
พริกชี้ฟ้าเขียว แดง โขลก	1	ช้อนโต๊ะ
พริกขี้หนูสับ	1/2	ช้อนชา
กระเทียมสับ	1	ช้อนโต๊ะ
กะเพราเด็ดเป็นใบ	4	ถ้วย
พริกไทยป่น	1/2	ช้อนชา
น้ำตาลทราย	1	ช้อนโต๊ะ
ซีอิ๊วขาว	1/2	ช้อนโต๊ะ
น้ำปลา	1/2	ช้อนโต๊ะ
น้ำมัน	1/4	ถ้วย

วิธีทำ

1. ใส่น้ำมันในกระทะ ใช้ไฟแรง พอน้ำมันร้อน ลดไฟลง ใส่ใบกะเพราครึ่งหนึ่งลงทอดเร็ว ๆ นำขึ้นผึ่งบนกระดาษซับน้ำมัน ทิ้งไว้ให้เย็น
2. นำน้ำมันที่ทอดใบกะเพราตั้งไฟกลาง พอร้อน ใส่กระเทียม พริกชี้ฟ้า พริกขี้หนู พริกไทย ผัดจนหอม ใส่แฮมลงผัด
3. ปรุงรสด้วยน้ำตาล ซีอิ๊วขาว น้ำปลา ใส่ใบกะเพราที่ยังไม่ได้ทอด ผัดพอใบกะเพราสุก ใส่ข้าวลงผัดให้เข้ากัน
4. ตักใส่จาน โรยใบกะเพราทอดกรอบ เสิร์ฟ

Khao Phat Kra-thiam

Garlic fried rice

ข้าวผัดกระเทียม

Ingredients

1 cup cooked rice
1 tbsp. small pieces of shiitake mushroom
1 tsp. chopped garlic
1 tbsp. sliced garlic
1 tbsp. light soy sauce
3 tbsp. cooking oil
cucumber, carot, onion.

Preparation

1. Put the oil in a wok and heat. When it is hot, put in the chopped garlic, saute until golden.
2. Put the rice into the wok and stir fry. Add the mushroom and mix everything together well.
3. Season with the soy sauce. Add the sliced garlic, and continue stir frying until the garlic is done.
4. Dip up onto a plate, and serve hot with the cucumber, carrot and spring onion.

เครื่องปรุง

ข้าวสวย	1 ถ้วย
เห็ดหอมหั่น	1 ช้อนโต๊ะ
กระเทียมสับ	1 ช้อนชา
กระเทียมหั่นขวางตามกลีบ	1 ช้อนโต๊ะ
ซีอิ๊วขาว	1 ช้อนโต๊ะ
น้ำมัน	3 ช้อนโต๊ะ

แตงกวา แครอท ต้นหอม

วิธีทำ

1. ใส่น้ำมันในกระทะ ตั้งไฟให้ร้อน ใส่กระเทียมเจียวพอเหลือง
2. ใส่ข้าวลงผัด ใส่เห็ดหอม ผัดให้เข้ากัน
3. ปรุงรสด้วยซีอิ๊วขาว ใส่กระเทียมสด ผัดจนกระเทียมสุก
4. ตักใส่จาน เสิร์ฟกับแตงกวา แครอท ต้นหอม

Khao Yam Tha-le

Sour and spicy seafood and rice salad

ข้าวยำทะเล

Ingredients

1 cup cooked rice
5 shelled white prawns
1 squid, cut into bite-size pieces
1 tbsp. boiled crab meat
1 Chinese soup celery stalk, coarsely chopped
10 crushed hot chillies
1 tbsp. finely sliced shallot
1 tbsp. crisp-fried shallot slices
1 tbsp. sauted garlic
2 tbsp. horapha sweet basil leaves
1 tbsp. lime juice
1-2 tbsp. fish sauce

Preparation

1. Immerse the prawns and the squid in boiling water until done.
2. Mix the rice, chillies, crab meat, squid, and prawns together.
3. Season with fish sauce and lime juice. Add the shallot. Mix together well, transfer to a platter, sprinkle with basil, celery, shallot, and garlic, and serve.

เครื่องปรุง

ข้าวสวย	1	ถ้วย
กุ้งแชบ๊วย	5	ตัว
ปลาหมึกหั่นชิ้นพอคำ	1	ตัว
เนื้อปูต้ม	1	ช้อนโต๊ะ
ขึ้นฉ่ายหั่น	1	ต้น
พริกขี้หนูโขลก	10	เม็ด
หอมแดงซอย	1	ช้อนโต๊ะ
หอมแดงเจียว	1	ช้อนโต๊ะ
กระเทียมเจียว	1	ช้อนโต๊ะ
โหระพาเด็ดใบ	2	ช้อนโต๊ะ
น้ำมะนาว	1	ช้อนโต๊ะ
น้ำปลา	1-2	ช้อนโต๊ะ

วิธีทำ

1. ลวกกุ้ง ปลาหมึกให้สุก ใส่กระชอนไว้
2. เคล้าข้าวสวย พริกขี้หนู เนื้อปู ปลาหมึก กุ้ง เข้าด้วยกัน
3. ปรุงรสด้วยน้ำปลา น้ำมะนาว หอมแดง เคล้าให้เข้ากัน ตักใส่จาน โรยใบโหระพา ขึ้นฉ่าย หอมเจียว กระเทียม เสิร์ฟ

Khao Phat Sai Khai

Fried rice with egg

ข้าวผัดใส่ไข่

Ingredients

2 cups cooked rice
3 tbsp. small thin slices of pork left on
1 hen's egg
1 onion, sliced
1 tbsp. chopped garlic
1 tsp. sugar
1-2 tbsp. fish sauce
2 tbsp. cooking oil

Preparation

1. Heat the oil in a wok. When it is hot, fry the garlic until fragrant, and then add the pork and stir fry. When they are about done, add the onions, and stir fry together.
2. Season with the sugar and fish sauce, and mix well.
3. Put in the rice and fry with the other ingredients. Then, break the egg into the wok, mix well with the rice, and when done, dip up onto a plate. Serve with slices of cucumber, cabbage, lime, and half lime.

เครื่องปรุง

ข้าวสวย	๒ ถ้วย
เนื้อหมูหั่นชิ้นบางเล็ก	๓ ช้อนโต๊ะ
ไข่	๑ ฟอง
หอมใหญ่หั่นเสี้ยว	๑ หัว
กระเทียมสับ	๑ ช้อนโต๊ะ
น้ำตาลทราย	๑ ช้อนชา
น้ำปลา	๑-๒ ช้อนโต๊ะ
น้ำมัน	๒ ช้อนโต๊ะ

วิธีทำ

1. ใส่น้ำมันในกระทะ ตั้งไฟให้ร้อน ใส่กระเทียมเจียวให้หอม ใส่หมู ผัดให้เข้ากัน ใส่หอมใหญ่ ผัดให้ทั่ว
2. ปรุงรสด้วยน้ำตาล น้ำปลา ผัดให้ทั่ว
3. ใส่ข้าวลงผัดเข้าด้วยกัน ต่อยไข่ใส่ ผัดเคล้าให้ทั่ว พอสุกตักใส่จาน เสิร์ฟกับแตงกวา กะหล่ำปลี และมะนาวผ่าซีก

Khao Tom Pla Meuk

Squid and rice soup

ข้าวต้มปลาหมึก

Ingredients

1 cup cooked rice
200 grams squid
1 Chinese soup celery stem, cut into short pieces
1 tsp. sauted garlic
1 tsp. dried salted vegetables
1/2 tsp. ground galangal
1/4 tsp. ground pepper
1-2 tsp. light soy sauce
2 cups soup stock

Preparation

1. Wash and clean the squid, cut it into the bite-size pieces, and immerse in boiling water until done.
2. Place the stock and the rice in a pot and boil.
3. Season the soup with the soy sauce, stir well, and then turn off the heat. Dip the soup into a bowl. Add the squid, sprinkle with the dried salted vegetable, galangal, garlic, celery, and pepper, and serve.

เครื่องปรุง

ข้าวสวย	1	ถ้วย
ปลาหมึกกล้วย	200	กรัม
ขึ้นฉ่ายหั่นหยาบ	1	ต้น
กระเทียมเจียว	1	ช้อนชา
ตังฉ่าย	1	ช้อนชา
ข่าป่น	1/2	ช้อนชา
พริกไทยป่น	1/4	ช้อนชา
ซีอิ๊วขาว	1-2	ช้อนชา
น้ำซุป	2	ถ้วย

วิธีทำ

1. ล้างปลาหมึกให้สะอาด หั่นชิ้นพอคำ ลวกให้สุก
2. ใส่น้ำซุปลงในหม้อ ใส่ข้าว ตั้งไฟให้เดือด
3. ปรุงรสด้วยซีอิ๊วขาว คนพอทั่ว ปิดไฟ ตักใส่ชาม ใส่ปลาหมึก โรยตังฉ่าย ข่าป่น กระเทียมเจียว ขึ้นฉ่าย พริกไทย เสิร์ฟ

Khao Tom Pla

Red snapper and rice soup

ข้าวต้มปลา

Ingredients

1 cup cooked rice
200 grams red snapper meat
1 spring onion, thinly sliced
1 Chinese soup celery stem, cut into short lengths
1 tsp. sauted garlic
1 tsp. dried salted vegetables
1/2 tsp. ground galangal
1/4 tsp. ground pepper
1-2 tsp. light soy sauce
2 cups soup stock
sliced spur chilli in vinegar, ground fermented soybeans

Preparation

1. Cut the fish into bite-size pieces and immerse these in boiling water until done.
2. Place the stock and the rice in a pot and boil.
3. Season the soup with the soy sauce, stir well, and then dip into a bowl. Add the red snapper meat, sprinkle with the dried salted vegetable, galangal, garlic, celery, and pepper, and serve with the chilli in vinegar and fermented soybeans.

เครื่องปรุง

ข้าวสวย	1	ถ้วย
เนื้อปลากะพงแดง	200	กรัม
ต้นหอมซอย	1	ต้น
ขึ้นฉ่ายหั่นหยาบ	1	ต้น
กระเทียมเจียว	1	ช้อนชา
ตังฉ่าย	1	ช้อนชา
ข่าป่น	1/2	ช้อนชา
พริกไทยป่น	1/4	ช้อนชา
ซีอิ๊วขาว	1-2	ช้อนชา
น้ำซุป	2	ถ้วย

พริกชี้ฟ้าดอง เต้าเจี้ยวบด

วิธีทำ

1. หั่นเนื้อปลาเป็นชิ้นพอคำ ลวกให้สุก ใส่ชามไว้
2. ใส่น้ำซุปลงในหม้อ ใส่ข้าว ตั้งไฟให้เดือด
3. ปรุงรสด้วยซีอิ๊วขาว คนพอทั่ว ตักใส่ชามปลา โรยตังฉ่าย ข่าป่น กระเทียมเจียว ต้นหอม ขึ้นฉ่าย พริกไทยป่น รับประทานกับพริกชี้ฟ้าดองและเต้าเจี้ยวบด

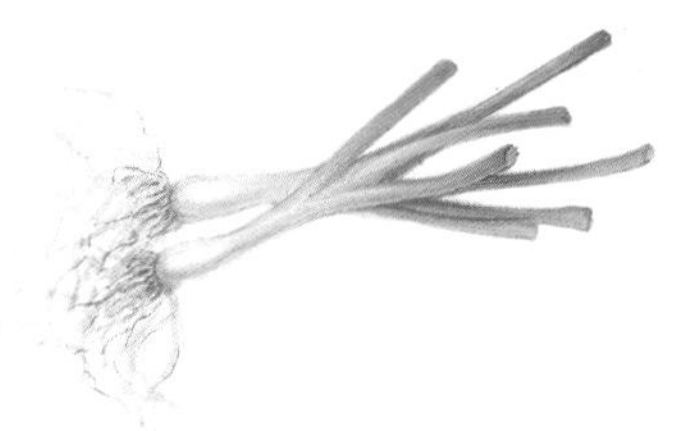

Khao Tom Si-Khrong Mu Seng Ji

Sparerib, kidney, and rice soup

ข้าวต้มซี่โครงหมูเซ่งจี๊

Ingredients

1 cup cooked rice
1 pork kidney
100 grams spareribs, cut into pieces
1 tsp. dried salted vegetables
1/4 tsp. ground pepper
1 tbsp. sauted garlic
1 tbsp. chopped spring onion and coriander greens
3 tbsp. light soy sauce
2-3 cups soup stock

Preparation

1. Cut the kidney in half, remove the white membrane in the middle, and then wash well. Cut it into bite-size pieces, and then leave these to soak in water for 15 to 20 minutes.
2. Pour the stock into a pot and heat it to boiling. Put in the spareribs and boil them until tender. Now, add the rice, kidney, and soy sauce, boil a while longer, and then turn off the heat.
3. Dip the soup into a bowl and sprinkle with the dried salted vegetable, pepper, spring onion and coriander, and garlic.

เครื่องปรุง

ข้าวสวย	1	ถ้วย
เซ่งจี๊	1	อัน
ซี่โครงหมูสับเป็นชิ้น	100	กรัม
ตังฉ่าย	1	ช้อนชา
พริกไทยป่น	1/4	ช้อนชา
กระเทียมเจียว	1	ช้อนโต๊ะ
ต้นหอมผักชีซอย	1	ช้อนโต๊ะ
ซีอิ๊วขาว	3	ช้อนโต๊ะ
น้ำซุป	2-3	ถ้วย

วิธีทำ

1. ผ่าเซ่งจี๊ เลาะสาบขาวออก ล้างให้สะอาด หั่นชิ้นพอคำ แช่น้ำไว้ประมาณ 15-20 นาที
2. ใส่น้ำซุปลงในหม้อ ตั้งไฟให้เดือด ใส่ซี่โครงหมูต้มจนนุ่ม ใส่ข้าวสวย เซ่งจี๊ ซีอิ๊วขาว เดือดสักครู่ ปิดไฟ
3. ตักข้าวต้มใส่ชาม โรยตังฉ่าย พริกไทย ต้นหอม ผักชี กระเทียมเจียว

Khao Tom Phakkat Khao

Cabbage, sparerib, and rice soup

ข้าวต้มผักกาดขาว

Ingredients

1 cup cooked rice
1 tbsp. dried shrimp
1 head Chinese cabbage, shredded
1 tbsp. sauted garlic
4 tbsp. fish sauce
2 cups soup stock

Preparation

1. Pour the stock into a pot and heat it to boiling. Put in the spareribs and boil until tender. Then, add the dried shrimp and cabbage. When the cabbage is tender, add the rice.
2. Season with the fish sauce, boil a little while longer, remove from the heat, and sprinkle with the garlic.

เครื่องปรุง

ข้าวสวย	๑ ถ้วย
กุ้งแห้ง	๑ ช้อนโต๊ะ
ผักกาดขาวหั่นเป็นเส้น	๑ ต้น
กระเทียมเจียว	๑ ช้อนโต๊ะ
น้ำปลา	๔ ช้อนโต๊ะ
น้ำซุป	๒ ถ้วย

วิธีทำ

1. ใส่น้ำซุปลงในหม้อ ตั้งไฟให้เดือด ใส่กุ้งแห้ง ผักกาดขาว พอผักนิ่ม ใส่ข้าวสวย
2. ปรุงรสด้วยน้ำปลา เดือดอีกครั้ง ยกลง โรยกระเทียมเจียว

Khao Op Mo Din

Rice baked in an earthen pot

ข้าวอบหม้อดิน

Ingredients

1 cup cooked rice
150 grams bite-size pieces of pork
5 rice-straw mushrooms, cut in half
1 spring onion, cut into short pieces
1 red spur chilli, sliced diagonally
1 tbsp. shredded ginger
1 tsp. light soy sauce
1 tbsp. oyster sauce
1-2 tbsp. cooking oil

Preparation

1. Heat the oil in a wok. When it is hot, stir fry the pork and then add the ginger, mushrooms, and spring onions. Season with the oyster and soy sauces. When everything is done nicely, turn off the heat.
2. Add the rice and mix thoroughly. Transfer to a covered bowl, sprinkle with the pepper, put on the cover, and bake for between 5 and 8 minutes in an oven at 375° F. oven. Serve hot.

เครื่องปรุง

ข้าวสวย	1	ถ้วย
เนื้อหมูหั่นชิ้นพอคำ	150	กรัม
เห็ดฟางผ่าครึ่ง	5	ดอก
ต้นหอมหั่นท่อนสั้น	1	ต้น
พริกชี้ฟ้าแดงหั่นเฉียง	1	เม็ด
ขิงซอย	1	ช้อนโต๊ะ
ซีอิ๊วขาว	1	ช้อนชา
น้ำมันหอย	1	ช้อนโต๊ะ
น้ำมัน	1-2	ช้อนโต๊ะ

วิธีทำ

1. ใส่น้ำมันในกระทะ ตั้งไฟให้ร้อน ใส่หมูลงผัด ใส่ขิง เห็ดฟาง ต้นหอม ผัดพอทั่ว ปรุงรสด้วยน้ำมันหอย ซีอิ๊วขาว ปิดไฟ ยกลง
2. เคล้าข้าวสวยกับส่วนผสมข้อ 1 ให้เข้ากันทั่ว ตักใส่ในถ้วยอบ โรยพริกชี้ฟ้า นำเข้าอบไฟ 375° ฟ. ประมาณ 5-8 นาที เสิร์ฟร้อน ๆ

Khao Op Het

Rice baked with mushrooms

ข้าวอบเห็ด

Ingredients

2 cups cooked rice
200 grams rice-straw mushrooms cut in half
2 shiitake mushrooms, soaked in water and cut into sections
5 green beans, strings removed and cut into 1 c.m. lengths
1/4 cup small chunks of pineapple
1 tomato, cut into chunks
1/4 cup corn kernels
1/4 tsp. ground pepper
1 tsp. sugar
2 tbsp. light soy sauce
2 tbsp. vegetable oil

Preparation

1. Put the oil in a wok over high heat. When hot, put in the two types of mushrooms, and the beans, pineapple, tomato, and corn, and stir fry.
2. Season with the soy sauce and sugar, and when ready, turn off the heat.
3. Add the rice and mix thoroughly. Scoop into a baking dish, sprinkle with the pepper, and bake at 350° F. for about 10 minutes.

เครื่องปรุง

ข้าวสวย	2	ถ้วย
เห็ดฟางผ่าครึ่ง	200	กรัม
เห็ดหอมแช่น้ำจนนิ่ม หั่นเสี้ยว	2	ดอก
ถั่วแขกดึงเส้นข้างออกหั่น ขนาด 1 ซม.	5	ฝัก
สับปะรดหั่นสี่เหลี่ยม ลูกเต๋า	1/4	ถ้วย
มะเขือเทศหั่นสี่เหลี่ยม ลูกเต๋า	1	ลูก
เมล็ดข้าวโพด	1/4	ถ้วย
พริกไทยป่น	1/4	ช้อนชา
น้ำตาลทราย	1	ช้อนชา
ซีอิ๊วขาว	1-2	ช้อนโต๊ะ
น้ำมันพืช	2	ช้อนโต๊ะ

วิธีทำ

1. ใส่น้ำมันในกระทะ ตั้งไฟให้ร้อน ใช้ไฟแรง ใส่เห็ดฟาง เห็ดหอม ถั่วแขก สับปะรด มะเขือเทศ เมล็ดข้าวโพด ผัดสักครู่
2. ปรุงรสด้วยซีอิ๊วขาว น้ำตาลทราย ผัดให้ทั่ว ปิดไฟ
3. ใส่ข้าวสวย เคล้าพอทั่ว ตักใส่ภาชนะที่จะใช้อบ โรยพริกไทยป่น นำเข้าอบไฟ 350° ฟ. ประมาณ 10 นาที

Khao Phat Phak

Vegetarian fried rice

ข้าวผัดผัก

Ingredients

1 cup cooked rice
2 shiitake mushrooms, soaked in water and cut into small pieces
1 yard-long bean, cut into 1/4-inch lengths
1 tsp. diced carrot
1/2 cup diced yellow bean curd
1 tsp. sugar
2 tbsp. light soy sauce
2 tbsp. vegetable oil

Preparation

1. Heat the oil in a wok. Put in the rice and stir fry. Add the mushrooms, bean, carrot, and bean curd, and fry together, stirring and turning to mix.
2. Season with the sugar and soy sauce. When everything is ready. dip up onto a plate and serve with cucumber and lime.

เครื่องปรุง

ข้าวสวย	1	ถ้วย
เห็ดหอมแช่น้ำหั่นเสี้ยว	2	ดอก
ถั่วฝักยาวหั่นยาว 1/2 ซม.	1	ฝัก
แครอทหั่นสี่เหลี่ยม		
ลูกเต๋าเล็ก	1	ช้อนชา
เต้าหู้เหลืองหั่นสี่เหลี่ยม		
ลูกเต๋าเล็ก	1/2	ถ้วย
น้ำตาลทราย	1	ช้อนชา
ซีอิ๊วขาว	2	ช้อนโต๊ะ
น้ำมัน	2	ช้อนโต๊ะ

วิธีทำ

1. ใส่น้ำมันในกระทะ ตั้งไฟให้ร้อน ใส่ข้าวลงผัด ใส่เห็ดหอม ถั่วฝักยาว แครอท เต้าหู้เหลือง ผัดให้เข้ากัน
2. ปรุงรสด้วยน้ำตาล ซีอิ๊วขาว ผัดจนสุก ยกลงเสิร์ฟกับแตงกวา และมะนาว

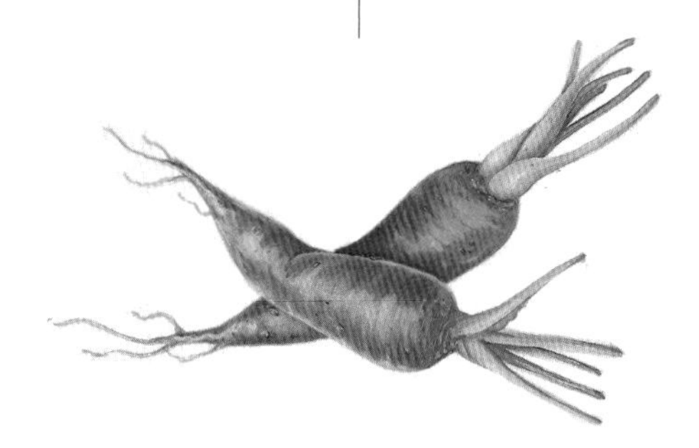

Printed in Thailand
Publisher and Distributor Sangdad Publishing Co.,Ltd.
320 Lat Phrao 94 (Town in Town)
Wang thonglang, Bangkapi, Bangkok. 10310
Tel. 538-7576, 538-2167, 538-5553
FAX : (662) 538-1499